OFF~HIGHWAY
AND
CONSTRUCTION
TRUCKS

The Ford Louisville has proved to be a popular chassis for the mounting of transit mixers.

OFF~HIGHWAY
AND
CONSTRUCTION
TRUCKS

ARTHUR INGRAM
and COLIN PECK

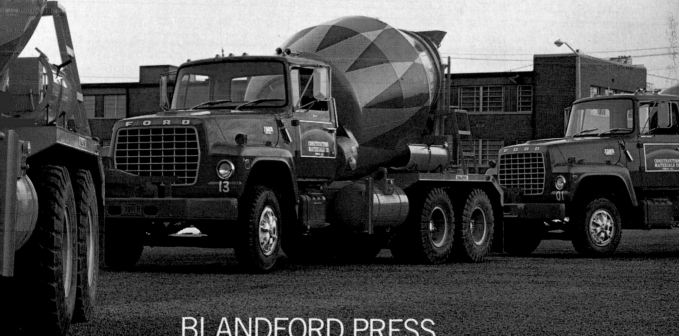

BLANDFORD PRESS
Poole　　　　Dorset

First published in the U.K. 1980

Copyright © 1980 Blandford Press Ltd
Link House, West Street, Poole,
Dorset BH15 1LL

British Library Cataloguing in Publication Data

Ingram, Arthur
    Off-highway trucks & construction vehicles.
    1. All terrain vehicles   2. Construction equipment
    I. Title
    629.22'4   TL235.6

ISBN 0 7137 0960 X

Set in 10/10½ point V.I.P. Plantin,
printed and bound in Great Britain by
Fakenham Press Limited, Fakenham, Norfolk

*Oshkosh Snogo rotating type snowplough for
highway use.*

CONTENTS

INTRODUCTION 6
THE DEVELOPMENT OF
CONSTRUCTION VEHICLES 10
   Dump trucks and loaders 32
   Highway construction 44
   Transit mixers 50
LIGHT OFF-HIGHWAY VEHICLES 56
DUMP TRUCKS: MAKES AND
SPECIFICATIONS 66
AIRCRAFT SERVICING VEHICLES 86

INDUSTRIAL AND COMMERCIAL
VEHICLES 103
   Logging 104
   Mining and quarrying 110
   Molten metal carriage 113
   Road/rail trucks 116
   Rubbish disposal 120
   Coal hauling 125
DRILLING RIGS 130
   Oilfield trucking 136
CRANES 143
TRUCK MODELS 152
ACKNOWLEDGEMENTS 158
INDEX 159

INTRODUCTION

The field of operation of an off-highway truck is completely different from that of its roadgoing counterpart. It is for this fundamental reason that the vehicle embodies certain design and construction features which set it apart from the more usual kind of truck.

As soon as any vehicle leaves that smooth ribbon of asphalt or concrete, it suffers in a number of ways. Because traction across unmade roads or even natural surfaces is more difficult than on the metalled road, the carrying capacity must be reduced if the vehicle is to maintain a reasonable performance. Alternatively, in order to achieve a constant capacity, the power may be increased.

Allied to the problem of traction is that relating to the type of tyres specified, because the comparatively high pressure highway type, with many shallow grooves designed to maintain a grip on smooth surfaces and to provide an escape for surface water, soon gets badly cut on rocks or rendered smooth by mud filling the tread. Therefore special-purpose tyres have been designed to cope with the problems of off-highway operation. These include the large section types with a chunky pattern of large cross ribs for cross country, the low pressure flotation types for swampy areas and the studded type for hard frozen surfaces.

Another aspect requiring attention is the gradient ability (or the hill-climbing capability) of the truck, remembering that the surface is not always constant as is the case with normal roads. This is where the gearbox and final drive ratios are important, for much of the work of the off-highway truck may be across hillsides, up quarry slopes or along forest tracks. Although the road speed is not of paramount importance the vehicle should not have to spend all day in bottom gear, for this could be very costly in fuel and could send the coolant temperature soaring.

The chassis frame and suspension are also of great significance, for these two items bear the brunt of the punishment handed out by rough surfaces. The very basis of the truck is its chassis frame, and for this reason it needs to be much stronger than those specified for highway use. Most truck chassis consist of a pair of parallel side rails tied together with a series of transverse cross members. The normal type of truck has pressed steel channel section side rails with similar type cross members placed at strategic intervals along

1

2

1. Magirus Deutz have been particularly successful in the on/off highway dump truck market with their 6×4 bonneted chassis.

2. The Foden Superhaulmaster 38 tonne tipper is the latest model in the on/off highway types produced by this maker.

3. In particularly arid regions the use of a water sprinkler makes operating conditions just that little bit more bearable.

the length of its chassis frame.

The actual dimensions of the U-section channel frame used are dependent upon the load which will eventually be superimposed on the frame. The frame specified for a 10 tonne gross van will obviously be unsuitable to put under a 30 tonne gross tipper.

Some manufacturers find it expedient virtually to 'add on' parts to a particular size of chassis frame in order to make it suitable for a higher capacity without having to resort to a completely different size of frame. These additions can take the form of lengths of flat steel bolted to the outside of the channel section; and these can be for the whole length of the frame or just the areas of greatest stress, such as around a rear bogie and its suspensions. Another system is to use a smaller section of steel channel on the outside of the main frame in the reverse direction, so that the resultant frame rail is an I-section made up of the U-sections bolted back to back. Yet another method is to weld up a complete box section.

Where greater strength is required and a fresh start can be made, as opposed to the fabricating techniques outlined above, structural steel beams are used in preference to the pressed steel channels. The structural steel can still be of channel section or an I-beam can be utilized; these are shaped by rolling during manufacture rather than by cold pressing which is the method used for the lighter frames.

Much of the strength of the chassis frame is dependent upon the actual depth or height of the side rails: the greater the height the greater the resistance to bending. Added to this is the bracing effect of the chassis cross members. These must be positioned at the places of greatest stress, such as the suspension anchorage points and bogie centres, to support a particular transmission item, as well as at the extreme ends of the frame. It must be remembered that these vehicles can be subjected to much pushing and pulling if they ever get stuck.

The truck suspension has the task of handling the irregularities in the surface traversed without subjecting the chassis frame to undue punishment and twisting. For a heavy dump truck the suspension will be reasonably hard, but for transporting fragile equipment something more flexible is required.

Clearance for the tyres has to be considered, for whereas 4 inches may be adequate for a roadgoing vehicle, something greater than this will be necessary for genuine cross-country vehicles. Most countries have regulations concerning the fitting of mudwings to vehicles on the highway; therefore, any vehicles fulfilling an on/off-highway role will have to be constructed so as not to breach current regulations. This also applies to all the other legislation regarding weights, length, width, lights and tyres, although temporary dispensation can be obtained, for instance, when vehicles are moving to a dock for export or where they merely have to cross the public highway in order to reach another part of a construction site. In order to meet the regulations concerning wings, some manufacturers have had to resort to the cycle type front wings, which are attached to the axle or hub assembly and not to the body. In this way the wing rises and falls with the wheel and a predetermined clearance can be maintained.

As mentioned above, many countries have enacted laws which carefully restrict the use of vehicles on the highway to certain parameters regarding size, weight, construction and use. It is often the very existence of these laws which sets the off-highway vehicle apart, for at the design stage it is realized that the payload or overall configuration demanded will place the completed vehicle far outside the boundaries of the regulations. This, therefore, is one way in which a vehicle can qualify for the 'off-highway' classification.

The actual section, diameter and tread of the tyres may also have to be considered, for the off-highway vehicle may have to come to grips with all manner of terrain. Large diameter wheels will increase the ground clearance under the axles. Large section tyres can take the place of twin tyres and so reduce the risk of rocks jamming between the tyres, as well as being capable of operating at lower pressures. For operation across sandy deserts, or even swamps, some very wide types are available which reduce the ground pressure even further to prevent the vehicle becoming bogged down. For extremely difficult situations a partially or totally tracked vehicle may be necessary. An air cushion arrangement can be useful for swamps or bogs. Tyre treads are controlled by the types of surface over which the vehicle will operate. Sandy regions demand the 'flotation' type of tyre with little lateral tread pattern, but for sticky soils a large chunky tread pattern with wide clevities between bars is required. This is also known as the 'trackgrip' or 'military' pattern.

Studded tyres have found use in areas covered by hard, frozen snow or ice, and chains or cleats are also used in some regions where the vehicle traverses different surfaces.

Additional features often specified for these vehicles include substantial towing hooks front and rear in case the vehicle has to be towed out. Some users require a winch to be fitted to the vehicle so that it can extricate itself from a sticky position, assuming that there is some form of anchorage available in the shape of a large tree or other heavy vehicle.

Heavy duty bumpers are also useful. These enable the vehicle to be pushed out of the way or even assisted up an incline by a bulldozer (which is not all that unusual an occurrence in some conditions).

When working in a quarry or other rocky area, the provision of under-chassis guards is sometimes prudent in order to avoid damage to the engine sump or brake gear. Another innovation is the fitting of small rollers to the underside of the axles to assist the movement of the truck over obstacles.

The 'route' of the vehicle exhaust system is another point which needs to be studied. In normal vehicles it is often taken *down* from the engine manifold, along below the frame and perhaps even across the chassis before discharging to the side. For a vehicle working in a quarry or a construction site, the exhaust system must be kept up, away from any possible damage either from rocks which will hole it or from mud which will probably remove the whole assembly!

Two considerations which are perhaps not so obvious are the position and size of the engine radiator. For a vehicle which is to operate in a hot climate, or one which moves slowly, a large cooling area is required and a large diameter fan to go with it. The radiator core should be kept free of obstructions and placed high up, or at least protected from possible damage by other vehicles, rocks or other obstacles.

Obviously, air-cooled engines do not suffer the vagaries of their liquid-cooled counterparts. This does not mean, however, that one can forget their cooling – far from it. One vehicle operator found to his cost that his air-cooled diesels suffered from overheating. Upon investigation it was found that a layer of fine particles had built up between the cooling fins, thus virtually excluding the stream of cooling air.

Another problem discovered with a water-cooled truck operating in dense grassland was that grass seeds were drawn into the radiator, effectively blocking the air stream. The remedy was to mount the radiator higher above the grass. Even this solution, however, may lead to danger, as one bus operator found with his fleet of rear-engined buses with side-mounted radiators. These had the water filler mounted so high that the drivers got very wet when trying to top up the header tank with a water can. The result was that no one could be bothered to check the water levels and the engines overheated. Even this would not have been so bad if the buses had been front-engined, for then any boiling would have been obvious.

Contrary to all that has been stated above is the case of the operation of vehicles in freezing conditions, for then a whole new set of problems arises. This is where the air-cooled diesel should score, because of the absence of any need for anti-freeze mixtures (but then the drivers complain that there is no comforting warmth from the engine!).

Naturally, far more problems arise with the operation of vehicles in sub-zero temperatures. These include fuel waxing, filters freezing, brake gear freezing up, ice forming on equipment, difficulty in starting and no one wishing to shut down the engine even for a meal break!

Another point concerning the crew is their safety and comfort. It is not unknown for cross-country vehicles to become overturned whilst traversing difficult areas, so the cab interior should be free of any sharp corners or spiky levers to injure the occupants should they be heaped together as the vehicle rolls over.

All loose equipment should be safely stowed, for something like a heavy lifting jack can be lethal if it is thrown about the cab as the vehicle rolls and pitches over rough ground. Safety belts or harness is necessary to keep the crew in their seats and prevent their heads being jolted against the roof, and safety helmets will also help in this direction. A good suspension seat will help iron out the bumps and adequate insulation, double glazing and an air conditioner will provide a better working environment.

THE DEVELOPMENT OF CONSTRUCTION VEHICLES

Construction vehicles and equipment have developed in parallel with their road-going counterparts, but have expanded in capacity and efficiency far beyond the expectation of operators.

Mechanization has taken place on a vast scale in order to maintain the progress and met the schedules demanded by such rapid expansion.

Smaller type of Caterpillar dump truck being used on highway construction at Milton Keynes New Town.

The construction industry is by far the greatest user of special transport equipment, and the list of vehicle types is almost endless. From the moment that a completely uninhabited area is chosen for development or a derelict building is scheduled for redevelopment until such work is completed there will be a connection with vehicles or transportable equipment of one kind or another.

The preparation of even a completely flat tract of land will need vehicles to deliver the site equipment and to bring men to carry out the work. A site office may well be required, and this will be delivered by road. A trenching machine could be used to dig the foundation trenches, which will have to be delivered to the site by low-loader if it is not self-propelled.

Should the project be a large one, perhaps surveyors, engineers and architects will need to study the area, possibly using a 4×4 truck. Then soil samples may be required or a water supply may need to be investigated, and a drilling rig hired to carry out these tasks. A stockpile of materials and fittings will be required to maintain schedules, and these may require the provision of special store areas, racks, dumps, bunds, tanks, silos, compounds and so on. A concrete batching plant may be installed, together with storage areas for the sand, aggregate, cement and water.

In order to provide good access for the constant stream of delivering vehicles it may be necessary to provide some kind of road or hard-standing area so that vehicles do not get bogged down. This can take the form of a temporary surface of old railway sleepers or aggregate; it may, alternatively, be advantageous to put in a proper road. On some sites the very first task is to put in the road system, so that good access is provided right from the start of the project.

If the site is remote from public transport systems, it may be necessary to provide space for vehicle parking or even to arrange a private bus service from the nearest railhead or airfield. Some large construction projects have entailed the use of

Mack LMSW 6×4 off-highway chassis with old style Jaeger transit mixer which used a horizontal cylindrical-shaped drum.

vast fleets of buses to ferry workers from the nearest towns. In some very remote areas it may be necessary to assemble a temporary site town made up of caravans or portable or prefabricated-type buildings for the large army of construction workers. Then follows the building of canteens, toilets, clubs, shops, first aid facilities and so on. All these facilities have to be brought to the site by vehicles of one kind or another, in addition to items of plant, vehicles for the supply of materials and items of specialist equipment.

All this is based on the assumption that the site is a reasonably easy one with regard to level, surface, altitude and climate. It may well be that the site for a hydro-electric scheme is on a mountainside with a restricted road system, and indeed access may be nigh impossible. It may be reasonably easy for the surveyors to get there by 4×4 or even by helicopter, but the problems associated with moving in all the heavy plant and the vast quantities of ready-mixed concrete, steel piling or reinforcing rods, sand and aggregate, timber for shuttering, large diameter pipes and so on are somewhat daunting. The final straw comes when the site is ready to receive the large pieces of electrical equipment and chunky generators or transformers have to be delivered and installed. Often new roads have to be provided, for the combined weight of the load and the vehicle is considerable.

Other problems have to be overcome when the site chosen has to be cleared of rocks and trees, or just levelled. In some instances a river may have to be temporarily diverted while the project is in hand. Road diversions or closures are quite common in large projects and even in some small ones.

Altitude can affect the project in several ways. The height of the site can make access difficult, and in very high locations the weather may be adverse. In some instances, also, the output of men and vehicles can be lowered by the effect of the rarefied air.

The latitude and climate can make a great deal of difference to the working conditions encountered at the site. Obviously, laying a pipeline in a hot desert region involves problems different from those that will be met when carrying out a similar project, for example, in Alaska. Natural obstacles such as bogs or particularly hard strata of rock can render diversions necessary as well as requiring the use of additional equipment. In one part of the

1

2

1. The importance of a high tipping angle to ensure rapid clearing of the load is demonstrated by an Italian-built Perlini truck.

2. Terex model 33–07 dump truck being loaded by a dragline.

3. Dutch-built Terberg 8×8 on/off-highway type which uses Volvo cab and running units.

world, work may be brought to a halt because of
the rainy season, whereas in another the same
result may be caused by large falls of snow.

The construction industry, therefore, relies
heavily on specialist equipment designed for the
job, and much of this has only been made possible
by the development of power techniques in the
recent past.

During the major industrial expansion caused by
the railway building era of just over 100 years ago,
much of the construction work was carried out by
huge armies of navvies or labourers. These were
assisted by mule teams or horses, together with
small rail trucks, until the steam-powered and
rope-operated mechanical shovels came upon the
scene. The largest types of steam 'navvies', as they
were called, were rail-mounted, because the great
weights would have caused the machines to sink in
the soft earth of the construction site. The lighter
models were mounted on iron-spoked wheels.

*One of a batch of Scammell 8×6 snow
plough/gritters obtained for clearing the first stretch
of the London–Birmingham motorway.*

The perfection of the crawler or caterpillar track marked the next important step in technical advance in the early 1920s, after achieving military success in World War 1. The paraffin or petrol internal combustion engine was also being used to power excavators, and diesel-engined units naturally followed.

By far the greatest fillip to mechanical plant occurred with the perfection of the high pressure hydraulic ram. This really did not go into series production until after World War 2, although some hydraulic dozers were used during the war. This new method of powering and manipulation of mechanical plant enabled designers to produce much more sophisticated items of equipment than had been possible with the winch and rope systems used previously. At the outset, hydraulic systems had many critics, who felt that although hydraulics were suitable for light equipment they simply could not replace the earlier power system for the very big items of plant. During the past thirty years there has been considerable expansion of hydraulics, but as yet they have not been adopted for the very largest construction equipment.

Another important step in the aptitude of mobile equipment was the perfection of the giant pneumatic tyre. The use of these large section, low pressure tyres enabled construction equipment to perform with much greater alacrity than the old style of equipment with normal truck-size wheels and tyres. Although the large mobile tyres used on earthmovers and dumpers did not have the absolute tenacity of a tracked vehicle, they did nevertheless have certain advantages over what had become the established form of soft terrain movement. Today, the tracked vehicle forms the base for few items of equipment except in the very heavy sector of the industry. In everyday use tracked bases are generally limited to bulldozers, angledozers and tilt dozers for the excavation of bases for cranes, draglines, piledrivers, shovels and skimmers. Even in this sphere the tracked base is challenged by the wheeled variety, but each has its limitations, and site engineers have to make their choice in the light of experience.

In order to get an idea of the myriad of construction equipment in use, it is probably best to arrange the items into some semblance of order.

Bulldozers seem to have established themselves as the prime example of an item of heavy plant for

1

2

1. British-built DJB articulated dump truck being loaded by a Caterpillar tracked loader.

2. Many miles of Britain's trunk roads are cleared of snow by bladed ploughs such as this Foden 6×4 equipped with Atkinsons of Clitheroe gritting equipment.

3. Articulated low loaders are used for the movement of construction equipment. Trailers may be loaded by ramps, or by detaching the rear axle or the swan neck.

site clearance. First appearing in the 1920s as a fixed blade attached to a tracked tractor, the basic design was exploited by improving the system of blade control without the need for the driver to leave his seat. Electric drives and engine-powered rope systems have been used for blade control, but now hydraulics carry out the task. As mentioned earlier, the development of the giant pneumatic tyre helped to expand the scope of all types of construction equipment, and the bulldozer has benefited likewise.

Parallel to bulldozer development has been the small loading shovel expansion. This also originated in crawler-tracked form and later progressed into the wheeled variety. Not only do the large tyres make maintenance easier, but they also allow the machine to be driven over normal roads without fear of repercussions from highway authorities over damaged surfaces.

Later developments in loaders have included four-wheel drive, four-wheel steering, articulated chassis, automatic transmission and a second fitment enabling the implement to perform the dual function of a backacter and a loader.

The towed scraper has been in use for very many years, and has gone through various stages of development by being carried on heavy iron wheels, full tracks, truck type tyres and finally giant earthmoving type tyres. Early types were rather of the bucket shape and had no door, whereas later designs have provided a vehicle which will scrape the load into the bowl, carry it to a new site and spread it evenly by means of a movable barrier-type door. As with other related items of equipment the breed has been improved by the adoption of hydraulic power in place of earlier rope-operated controls.

Closely associated with the towed scraper is the motor scraper. This employs a single-axled powered tractor unit which is permanently coupled ahead of the scraper bowl.

Scrapers are employed where large areas of land can be lowered by the scraper taking shallow cuts over a long run. The wheeled variety, either powered or towed, can operate on most surfaces; but in very heavy sticky soils the towed variety with a crawler tractor is advisable.

For a much finer finish to the level site a grader is employed. This item of equipment uses an angled blade mounted across the frame of the machine in the centre. By judicious use of the levelling controls the operator can remove the slight undulations in the surface. The machine is also used to spread aggregate over a surface, prior to rolling. Some contractors additionally fit tines or scarifiers to graders and so increase their usefulness. Some designs have a fully adjustable blade which can be inclined at an angle toward the side for levelling a bank at the roadside; or the blade can be tilted down so that it can be used for making a roadside ditch.

Many of the larger items of digging and construction equipment all emanate from one basic design of chassis – the excavator base machine. This design is a fairly old one, and it consists of a rigid baseplate structure within a pair of crawler tracks. On the baseplate is mounted a turntable upon which is carried the machine's superstructure containing the power unit, winding gear and controls.

What most people understand to be an excavator is more accurately termed a 'face shovel'. It consists of the excavator base with a superstructure containing the power unit, including drums for the wire ropes together with all the clutches, gearing and controls necessary to the function of the machine. Additionally, there is the driver's cabin, which is glazed sufficiently for him to have a good view of the excavating operation and the loading of the trucks. A substantial counterbalance weight is positioned at the rear of the superstructure.

The bucket is mounted on a short, stiff bucket arm which is arranged to pivot about the centre point of the main boom. The bucket arm is also arranged to slide within the boom by means of a saddle block.

The face shovel is used for removing material which is above the level of the machine, and its mode of operation is to make upward cuts into the working and deposit the spoil into waiting trucks by swinging through an arc of between 30 and 120

1. *The use of mesh chains on all wheels has the dual function of providing better grip as well as protecting the tyres from damage.*

2. *Taskers twin-end dual loading trailer.*

1

2

1

2

3

1. *Volvo N1225 6×2 and drawbar trailer equipped with side tipping bodies and operated by a Danish contractor.*

2. *Volvo F and N series 6×4 dump trucks employed on stone quarrying in Sweden.*

3. *Terex 33–07 model dump truck undergoing demonstration trials for the Associated Portland Cement Manufacturers.*

4. *Old trucks never die! A World War 2 AEC Matador still hard at work in a Devon quarry.*

4

degrees. Discharging takes place by releasing the bucket door.

Naturally the machine works in a semicircle from a standing position and has to move to an adjacent part of the bank once all the material within reach has been removed. Alternatively, it can work parallel to the bank, gradually working along the bank laterally, as opposed to facing it squarely, and making a series of semicircular scoops in its face.

For removing soil below the standing level of the machine, a backacter is used. This implement has the bucket arranged on the end of a short bucket arm which is pivoted to the top end of the boom. The machine operates by raising the bucket arm out in front and making a sweep down and toward the base. With loaded bucket kept up and in toward the base the machine is swung round and the spoil deposited in the waiting truck by raising the bucket arm toward the horizontal. To avoid loss of load some models are fitted with a door to the bucket.

Another type of excavating base machine is the skimmer. This removes spoil by means of the bucket sliding along the boom, which is almost in a horizontal position. The bucket scoops the soil on its forward movement, the boom is raised and the contents are discharged by opening the bucket door at the rear. As the boom descends to the working position the bucket is returned to the base of the boom ready for the next cut.

For shallow excavations below base level but over a wider area, the dragline comes into use. This machine has a long lattice type boom with an open bucket hung from the end of the boom, but controlled by a cable attached to the mouth of the bucket and wound into the front of the superstructure.

The dragline is useful for making shallow cuts in soft soils, relying as it does purely on its own weight when cast out by the boom and dropped on the working. It is often used for clearing ditches or canals, dredging in swampy areas, or for removing soft materials where its long reach can be used to advantage so that the base stands on a firm foundation.

In action the bucket is cast out so that ideally it strikes the surface at a point below the end of the boom. The drag cable is then wound in and the bucket is filled as it is dragged toward the base. The

1

2

1. *Older style Euclid scraper with bowl open and soil being spread over road base.*

2. *Hy-Mac tracked hydraulic back-hoe being used to form the sides of a road cutting.*

3. *Early type of hydraulically controlled Caterpillar bulldozer.*

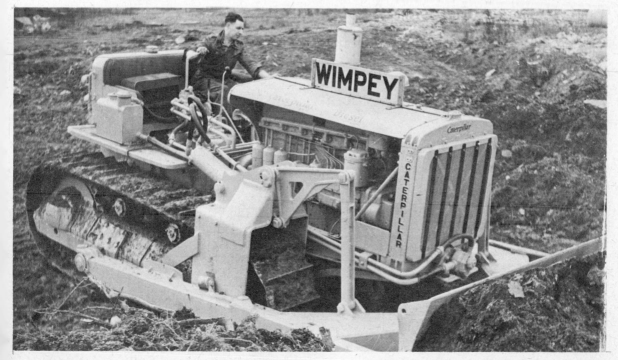

1

2

1. *Euclid B–70 articulated dumper with bottom discharge used on a refuse tip to spread soil over the garbage.*

2. *Terex model 33–15 being loaded by a 280–B Bucyrus Erie shovel at the Empire Iron Mining Company.*

3. *Aveling Barford 4×2 followed by a Moxy D153 six wheeler at work on a road construction project.*

3

bucket is tilted by action of the dump cable, the boom swung round and the spoil discharged by tilting the bucket with the dump cable. The dragline then returns to its original position and the sequence is repeated.

The excavator base machine is also used for mounting lifting cranes and for clamshell-type cranes or excavators, drop hammers, pile drills and pile drivers.

All the machines mentioned above are of the older rope-operated type. Many of the construction machines used today, however, are of the hydraulic type, which offers certain advantages with regard to greater capacities (without having to resort to unduly large fabrications), greater power of action and a greater degree of flexibility in operation. The control of these machines is much more precise, with the result that operator training is quicker and the work is finished to finer limits.

Most popular of the hydraulic units are the back hoes, face shovels and bucket excavators. These can also be adapted as cranes or concrete breakers. There are many optional fixtures available to the contractor so that the basic machine can be adapted for a variety of tasks by the addition of special grabs, buckets, tines, rippers or ditching tools.

For sites which are not too difficult, most of the equipment mentioned above may be used with a wheeled base as opposed to the heavier crawler-tracked type. The wheeled base is far more mobile and can often be towed or driven along the highway instead of having to be low-loaded like the tracked variety.

One disadvantage of the wheeled type of site vehicle is its lack of adhesion in comparison with tracked vehicles. It is not really able to tackle heavy excavation, root pulling or scarifying, because wheelspin may occur. It is ideally suited to work on hard or reasonable surfaces, or where there is a long run between loading and discharge points.

The tracked vehicle is more at home on difficult, sticky surfaces, and can turn in a small space because of its reversible or braked tracks system of steering. On the other hand, some wheeled loaders are of articulated construction, thus making for improved manoeuvrability, although this is still not comparable to the immediate 'about face' possible with tracked machines.

Smallest of the loaders, excavators, back hoes and diggers are those derived from the earliest mechanical shovels based on agricultural tractor designs. Many of these small machines are easily recognizable because of their tractor-like outline, but others have become enlarged and improved, rendering their parentage less obvious.

Usually, the tractor-based designs still cling to the large driving wheels and small steering wheels arrangement. The larger models, however, have opted for large wheels all round, with perhaps four-wheel drive, articulated layout or four-wheel steering arrangement.

For small projects, these little vehicles are called upon to carry out a whole host of tasks, so there is a wide selection of optional fittings. In many instances they are fitted with a back hoe and a loading shovel at the front. As the whole unit is rather on the lightweight side, hydraulic stabilizers provide greater adhesion, and some operators lower the loading bucket in order to raise the wheels completely off the ground.

There is one type of loader which loads the shovel at the front of the machine by driving into the load, and then reverses toward the truck to be loaded and discharges by hoisting the bucket up over the cab and tipping the contents. This saves time because the complete loader does not have to be turned for each bucket of load.

The tractor-derived machines are invaluable to the small site contractor, and they have achieved great success with road repairing, service industries and local authorities. They can be seen clearing ditches, digging trenches, lifting equipment, loading trucks, moving logs and pipes, clearing snow, scarifying, site clearing and hole boring; in fact almost all the lighter jobs are within their range.

1. Ruston Bucyrus excavator base machine rigged as a dragline, at work alongside a partially complete stretch of highway.

2. A much larger Marion 7400 dragline working in the confines of a quarry where it is used to bring material up to loading level for the smaller face shovel seen in the distance.

1

2

1. Rare among construction vehicles are the
Canadian-built Rubber Railway rigid eight
wheelers which are steered by pivoting of the front
bogie.

2. The rigid eight wheel chassis is finding greater use
by European operators for the mounting of transit
mixers. This MAN is used by a Dutch cement
producer.

3. The Mack DM series was so designated because
it was specifically designed for the Dumper and
Mixer bodies widely used in the construction
industry.

DUMP TRUCKS AND LOADERS

Dump trucks, or dumpers, have developed from different sources. The small site dumpers are really the modern counterparts of the wheelbarrow, whereas the large capacity dump trucks started out as tipper trucks.

In the early days of construction work, much of the material to be moved was dug out by hand and carried away in baskets or carts. Narrow gauge railway tracks were also laid, and railway trucks were pushed and pulled by men, horses or steam-power. On many smaller construction projects, however, the handbarrow was deemed sufficient to remove the spoil and carry the building materials. With the limitation on the weight that can be managed by one man, a whole army of labourers was necessary to keep up regular movement of materials on the site, and for this reason the motor vehicle was tried. Unfortunately a construction site is not the best place for a normal vehicle, for a number of reasons, the major ones being the absence of any proper surface and the fact that most sites are generally littered with equipment and workings which render the free movement of vehicles impossible.

Small site dumpers

The resulting site dumper had to be quite small in size, which also meant that its capacity was limited. The latter is no great disadvantage, because quite often the amounts to be moved can be arranged in small lots spread over a large area as the work progresses. It is usually only in the early stages of clearing or levelling a site that large quantities of soil or rock are required to be moved, and then the site is free of actual works and there is room for the larger vehicles to manoeuvre.

The early site dumpers, therefore, were based on farm tractors with a hand-tipped body of a capacity of perhaps 1 or 2 cubic yards. Later on, lighter designs appeared with the development of large section pneumatic tyres of the 'cross-country' type, which provided the dumpers with greater ability to handle site conditions without fear of becoming

A Nord-Verk model TT 140B articulated dump truck is a Swedish design using a Volvo engine. It is also available as a cross-country truck and ISO container carrier.

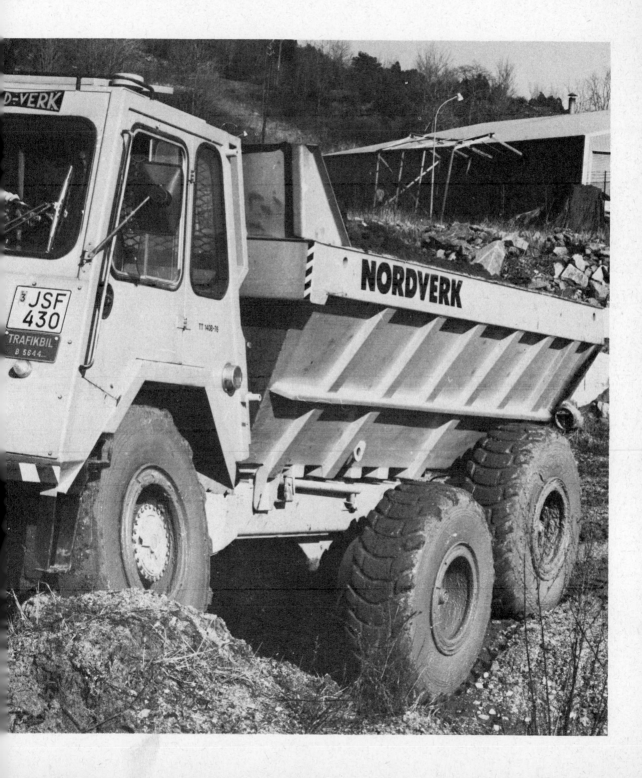

The Thwaites Alldrive 5-ton site dumper features all-wheel-drive and steering.

bogged down. More recent developments have included articulated designs for greater flexibility on undulating ground, hydraulic drive for the smoother application of power, and four-wheel drive for better adhesion in adverse conditions. Although some site dumpers can be obtained in large capacities, most types retain the original 'wheelbarrow' concept of light, small-size vehicles of good manoeuvrability with the attribute of being generally handy around the site. Whereas most are supplied with a general purpose scow-ended body which can be tipped to 90 degrees, and are used for earth, bricks, aggregate, rubble or indeed anything at all, there are some operated with a special semi-enclosed body for the better handling of wet concrete. A lip at the top of the otherwise open body helps prevent the loss of wet concrete mix on a rough site.

FORK TRUCKS

Another recent development closely allied to that of the site dumper is that of the rough terrain fork truck. This is rather a cross between the normal industrial fork truck and a site dumper. Over the

last thirty years the industrial fork-lift truck has revolutionized the handling and storage of a whole variety of goods. Through diversification it has been responsible for a whole new industry of mechanical handling which has helped most industries both to reduce labour costs (by speedier and more efficient loading/unloading of vehicles and transfer of goods and materials from and to production lines) and to perform countless warehousing and internal works functions. From the early designs of pure lifting devices, the fork truck has been developed into a real handling device which can lift, carry, position, lower, stack, retrieve, load and unload. By means of further detail designs it has widened its applications from the original concept of a fork-lift pallet truck. Now it can handle logs, cable drums, reels of paper, rolls of carpet,

The wheeled loader is a speedy machine able to handle a variety of loads in stockyards.

ISO containers and so on by means of clamps, forks, spigots and other specialist accessories.

In most of the above applications for fork trucks the truck is used on a good, hard and sometimes level surface – the direct opposite to normal conditions on a construction site. So the major problems to be overcome in producing a fork truck for site work are those relating to stability and traction. The small wheels and close ground clearance of the industrial truck are useless on a muddy site, so the site truck must have large wheels and ample under-axle clearance if it is to survive in sticky conditions.

Another variation on the light site dumper theme has been the design which employs a demountable skip-type body, of a capacity of around 2 cubic yards, which can be picked up by the carrying unit. The carrying frame unit is provided with lifting arms which connect with the skip and lift it on to the carrier. The same lifting arrangement can be used to tip the load or to deposit the skip anywhere on site, but the amount of lift is limited. This type of truck is in no way as flexible as the fork-lift truck for site work.

Other variations on the fork truck theme which are used on construction sites include a tipping type loading bucket which is attached in place of the forks, and can be used to place materials on say a first floor level. Another variation is for a non-tipping deep bucket which is carried between the forks, or a shallow metal mortar pan which is supported on the forks.

Further special adaptions which have been designed include a small capacity concrete mixer drum, a concrete skip of the type normally handled by a crane, and a small dumper type body mounted on a frame to coincide with the width of the fork spacing.

As with all other items of equipment constant vigilance is required with regard to safety when fork trucks are used on a busy site.

1

2

3

1. Design of self-loading concrete mixer which features rear control for accurate positioning of the load when tipping.

2. The ubiquitous Unimog equipped with a dozer blade for light site clearance duties.

3. The Clark Bobcat with its Ford engine and hydrostatic drive is one of the new generation small site loaders.

LARGE SITE DUMPERS

At the other end of the scale from the little site dumpers which can be seen scurrying about on construction sites, there are the much more impressive large dump trucks. These vehicles carry out a wide range of carrying and dumping jobs on sites, and are available in a variety of payload sizes. By the very virtue of the job they can perform, it is often difficult to distinguish one from another, for they invariably have similar scow-ended bodies, are built along established lines and are frequently painted the same colour! These features often render accurate identification difficult, especially from a distance, and the very size of the larger models can be misleading when viewed from the edge of a large site. It is not until a man or a normal vehicle is seen alongside one of these giants that the scale of the subject can really be appreciated.

When did these larger dumpers first appear? Well, it is generally accepted that the development has been gradual and that the first site dumpers were really just roadgoing trucks relegated to site work. Before the motor truck was sufficiently developed, earthmoving projects, quarrying and the like were handled by men, horses and rail trucks.

During the 1920s the heavy motor truck was beginning to be adopted almost universally in the United States, because there was no widespread use of heavy steam vehicles as existed in Britain. Therefore many contractors turned to the heaviest chassis available, and used strong bodies to remove spoil from building sites as well as to deliver the materials. The American heavy trucks were ahead of those manufactured in many other countries, and the production of the 10-ton payload Hewitt coal truck in 1909 was a milestone in truck development. This was not the usual size of truck, however, for on both sides of the Atlantic a payload of about 4 tons was much more the rule of the day. Nevertheless, it does show that US truck builders could produce high capacity vehicles if required;

The British DJB dump truck uses Caterpillar engine, transmission and axles, and is marketed through Caterpillar dealers.

although one fears to guess what their unladen weight was with the heavy frames, axles and wheels of the period.

Nevertheless, by dint of experience and experimentation, the site truck developed in two directions: firstly as a specialized offshoot of the normal highway truck; and secondly as the more specialized articulated or tractor-hauled dump trailer.

Taking the development of the truck-derived dump truck, we find firstly that these can conveniently be divided into highway types and site (or off-highway) types. As with many other transport functions there has to be a certain amount of flexibility, and vehicles are often designated as on/off-highway dumpers or tippers. This means that they have certain qualities rendering them suitable for

specific site jobs, while retaining their ability to fulfil highway operation criteria with regard to construction and use regulations in respect of size and weights, lighting, wings etc.

Generally speaking, the on/off-highway truck differs from a normal roadgoing vehicle in that it is able to enter and traverse unmade areas with a load. Naturally there are limits to its site capabilities, especially in bad weather, although to see the places where site agents want their bricks delivered sometimes leaves one doubting the fact! It is primarily the truck suspension and transmission which takes the brunt of the punishment in site operation, although the chassis frame itself comes in for some pretty bad treatment. Attempting to tip a load on an uneven surface is fraught with danger and it is not uncommon for the whole vehicle to

turn over. The frameless type of articulated tipper is particularly prone to this failure, especially if a sticky load does not clear the body rapidly as the angle of tip increases.

The body of the vehicle should be strongly fabricated to stand up to the battering received during loading by a mechanical shovel or excavator. It should have ample strengthening ribs at the sides to prevent bulging. The top edge should be reinforced by a box section, or something similar, to resist blows by the loading bucket. The front of the body should extend forward at least far enough to cover the gap between cab and body, and in some instances even further forward to protect the roof of the cab, for if heavy rocks are being loaded there is a possibility that one might fall on the cab roof, with disastrous results.

The inside of the body should be completely smooth for the rapid discharge of the load when tipped; and the angle of tip is important when dealing with loads of sticky clay. The scow end at the rear of the body should provide sufficient slope to contain the load across a bumpy site, but if the angle is too sharp it will negate a high tipping angle.

Most site dump trucks are of the rear tipping type. There are, however, some side tipping designs, though these are usually found in quarries where the site has been laid out on a more permanent basis than the construction site or road-building project. Another type is that with bottom discharge. This is not in widespread use in Britain, but finds greater potential in aggregate hauling in North America.

At one time the trailer type of dump truck was

Caterpillar 966C wheeled loader busily filling an Oshkosh on/off-highway dump truck engaged on a Middle East contract.

used behind a crawler-type tractor, and today some contractors use the articulated form of dump truck, though they are still very much in the minority.

Construction site dump trucks are usually of medium capacity (even those for large projects). The open-cast mine and large-scale quarries are the homes of the really big models. In a continuous production centre such as a strip mine, the scale of the undertaking is so large that it is economic to invest huge sums of money in the really big equipment. Everything is done on a grand scale with perhaps large walking draglines or bucket wheel excavators working round-the-clock shifts in order to justify their fantastic cost. The spoil is carried away by 100-tonne dump trucks or by long snaking conveyors direct to the crushing or screening plants, before being fed into mile upon mile of waiting railroad trucks.

Because of the temporary nature of a construction site there is not the same economy of scale of equipment as is possible with the permanent mine or quarry, and so everything is carried out in a much more easily handled size. The dump trucks are usually within the 10 to 50 tonne bracket, so that when the contract is complete the equipment can be moved to another site or sold off. With more everyday equipment the unit cost is lower and any lull between contracts should not send the contractor into bankruptcy.

Some contractors use the more custom-built dump trucks only when absolutely necessary on the more difficult sections of a site. For the more easy areas a fleet of more ordinary tippers will be pressed into service. Often such trucks first saw the light of day as highway-going vehicles, but after good service they were relegated to site work in the face of the stringent road traffic regulations. Many old tippers end their days on site work where they are run into the ground as the project progresses. Often the contract price will have been negotiated bearing in mind the fact that the fleet of trucks will have no useful life beyond the end of the project, and their value will be written off on that particular job. In some cases site dump trucks are hired from a supplier who is quite happy to extend the useful life of older vehicles without having to resort to expensive updating in the light of further legislation. (For further details, see chapter on Dump Trucks: Makes and Specifications.)

1

2

1. Foden off-highway dump truck on display at the annual Site Equipment Demonstration at Hatfield where the latest in construction equipment is exhibited.

2. Aveling Barford produce graders, loaders and rollers in addition to a series of dump trucks. They are within the Special Products division of British Leyland.

3. The ability of the wheeled loader to perform in confined spaces is demonstrated in this view of a Swiss Saurer articulated tipper being loaded.

HIGHWAY CONSTRUCTION

One of the most obvious places to find off-highway equipment at work is where a highway is under construction. Recent road-building programmes have meant the spending of vast sums of public money, and have demanded that adequate planning and sufficient equipment is on hand so that the programme can be followed and expensive delays avoided.

Modern highway construction is a long-term project and one which entails a great deal of study and planning before the first spadeful of earth is dug. With the high cost of land in the industrial nations there is much work to do even before the first lines are drawn on the map. Many factors have an influence on the route decided for a new road, not least being the views of the people who will be affected by it in one way or another. There will be much discussion with the interested parties as to which route should be taken, and past vehicle movement studies will be checked in order to ascertain exactly where certain traffic originates. For a very long time roads used to connect one town with the next, but today they are purposely routed around towns.

Once the route has been agreed upon and the land secured, the construction and layout decided and the contracts signed, work can actually commence. Bridges are normally constructed first and then the stretches of road connected to them. Often junctions with other roads may have been provided during earlier improvements to existing roads, but this varies with individual circumstances.

Where the new road traverses large areas of almost flat and open country, the rate of construction will be comparatively swift and perhaps cheap; but where the route is through difficult terrain, such as marsh, hard rock or very hilly areas, then work will of necessity be slower and more expensive. A waterlogged area may require draining or a lot of filling, or many piles may have to be sunk. Rocky areas will require drilling or blasting operations to clear the way or at least to provide cuttings for the road. Even in the comparative ease of a town, the high cost of land may require the road to be elevated above buildings or put down in a cutting or tunnel.

These requirements all mean additional work for the road-builders. Also to be taken into consider-ation is the weather, which can seriously hamper the work and add to the bill.

With a long stretch of road under construction, one might imagine that the contractors would start at one end and proceed to the other. However, where possible, work will be instigated at several points simultaneously, in order to complete the whole project within a reasonable time. The high-way authority might well insist on a tight schedule for the opening of the road to traffic, and any delays could incur financial penalties for the contractor. Also, in these days of inflation, any extension of the work could mean a vast increase in the cost of the whole project.

The actual vehicles and equipment used in road construction will naturally vary with the terrain

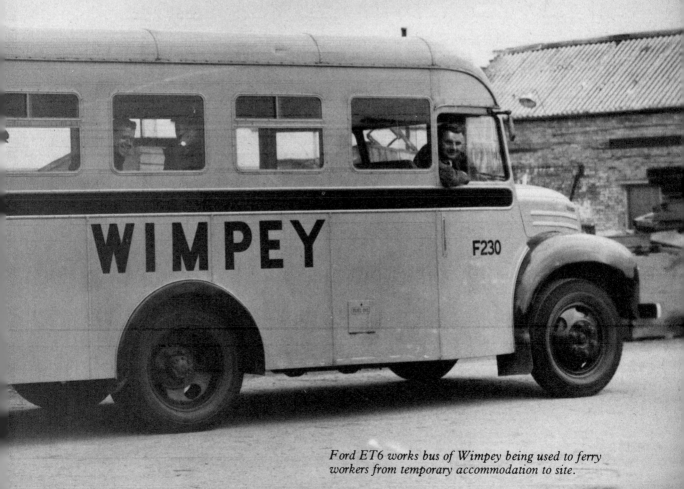

Ford ET6 works bus of Wimpey being used to ferry workers from temporary accommodation to site.

1

2

3

4

5

Views of work proceeding on a British Motorway project:

1. Bedford tipper delivering material to a batching plant.

2. Articulated scraper moving across an access 'road'.

3. Bridge supports in course of completion over an almost finished stretch of highway.

4. A grader profiling the slope of a cutting while scrapers level the bottom.

5. Articulated roller compacting the road base prior to the laying of the road stone and wearing surface.

Caterpillar dozer levelling material over a culvert on a road building project.

crossed and the amount of engineering works entailed in the project. Where the route covers soft yet stable open country, the normal series of scrapers, graders or skimmers should be adequate for preparing the site. Where more difficult ground has to be cleared, then heavier equipment will be required, including such items as bulldozers, face shovels, backacters, draglines, pile drills, pile drivers, excavators, rock drills and even blasting or tunnelling equipment.

Some of the vehicles and equipment required for road-building can proceed to the site on their own wheels; others may have to be transported to the site on low-loaders; and even larger items may require to be delivered in sections and assembled

on site. In this last category would come batching plants for concrete production, although some such plants can be obtained in a single unit which is mounted on a temporary bogie and fifth wheel plate for over-road transport by a tractor unit.

Another aspect of road-building work not always apparent is that of refuelling the site equipment, which is situated well away from existing highways. This demands a refuelling tanker which is able to traverse unmade roads in order to reach the equipment, and a 4×4 is normally sufficient. In many instances the construction vehicles are refuelled direct from the fueller, whereas in others the tanker delivers to a remote storage point and the site vehicles are refuelled there.

TRANSIT MIXERS

Although there has been considerable expansion in the use of transport concrete mixers in recent years, the basic idea is not new, for transit mixers existed in the steam wagon era. As one would expect, however, designs and capacities have changed and their use has become much more widespread.

The reasons for the great increase in the use of such equipment are speed and convenience. On small or congested sites there is often no room for an independent site mixing plant with its attendant storage areas. Particularly on crowded inner city sites where space is at a premium, it is so convenient to be able to dig the trenches, erect the shuttering and fix the reinforcing and then pour the concrete ready mixed straight from the transit mixer.

Oshkosh 8×8 transit mixer with low pressure tyres for delivering concrete under difficult conditions.

Obviously, the site must be adequately prepared to accept the physical size and weight of the mobile mixer. Provision must be made for the vehicle to gain access to the site itself and then to a point adjacent to that of the pouring operation. Earthworks should be reinforced to take the weight if the vehicle has to pass close by, and any new constructions must have had time to dry out before the heavy vehicle can pass over them. Once the pouring operation is under way it should be as continuous as possible; on a large ground area this may involve the use of a whole convoy of mixers arriving at predetermined times. If the vehicles are not able to discharge either directly on the pouring area or into a system of chutes, then the use of intermediate site dumpers will be necessary, and this will slow down the operation considerably. Another form of delay occurs when the concrete is required for constructing beams and columns, for the discharge cannot be completed so speedily.

If the concrete mix is required at a point remote from any vehicle access, even in places inaccessible to a site dumper or barrow, a concrete pumping unit is necessary. Concrete pumps consist of a vehicle chassis (equipped with a hopper to receive the concrete from the transit mixer), a powerful pump, a hydraulic boom and the piping necessary to transport the concrete to the required point.

The transit mixer can be used in three ways: by carrying a dry mix to the site and adding the water on arrival; by loading with the concrete partly mixed and then mixing it fully on arrival; or by taking on a fully mixed load and agitating it during transit.

Transit mixers are built in a variety of sizes to suit the amount of concrete required at a site at one time, yet maintaining loads within the road transport regulations of the country concerned. In Britain the tendency is for mixers to be of the 3 to 7 cubic metre capacity of wet mix, these being mounted on rigid vehicle chassis in the four-, six- or eight-wheel layout. In some European countries the use of a larger capacity mixing drum has resulted in articulated vehicles being specified, but these are limited to sites with good access and a substantial surface. North America favours the rigid chassis, with the number of axles being determined by the capacity of the mixer and the weight laws of the particular State in which the vehicle operates.

1

2

3

1. *The advantage of a front discharge mixer is clearly demonstrated in this view of footings being poured.*

2. *Foremost Forward transit mixer showing the elongated drum necessary to bring the load up over the cab.*

3. *The export-only Leyland Super Hippo chassis is used for these transit mixers used by Readymix on a contract in Israel.*

The transit mixer consists of the mixing drum, driving engine, water tank, loading hopper and discharge chute. In most instances the mix is loaded dry, the water added and the drum rotated to ensure a good mix and reduce the risk of premature hardening. Loading takes place from an overhead storage silo into the loading hopper placed high up at the mouth of the mixing drum. Inside the drum are convolute blades which act to agitate the mix as the drum is rotated in one direction by the engine, which drives the drum by gearing or chain. Upon arrival at the site, the drum is rotated in the opposite direction in order to discharge the mix into the chute and thence into a concrete pump hopper, concrete carrier or direct into the pouring area.

1. The Ford 6×4 chassis has found wide use as the basis for transit mixers in Britain.

2. In many European countries the larger capacity transit mixers used to be mounted on articulated vehicles, but now the trend is toward multi axle rigid chassis.

LIGHT OFF-HIGHWAY VEHICLES

Many believe that a war brings out the best in people because they are united against a common enemy. It is generally accepted that the jeep of World War 2 was the precursor of today's vast selection of light 4×4s, although it was not the first all-wheel-drive vehicle.

Schmidt type S lateral snowplough fitted to the ever-popular Unimog.

In the service industries there are a number of specialized vehicles used for a variety of particular purposes. Many of them fall into the on/off-highway class, for they are vehicles which can be used in or on such diverse areas as fields, stock-yards, docks, engineering works, construction sites, desert regions, mountainsides and even swampy areas. However, some will often work part-time on highways.

Naturally, the two main parameters when such vehicles are designed or specified are the function they are to fulfil and the terrain in which they will operate. Because these vehicles are so specialized, any generalizations are worthless, for each is custom-built for the job and no two are exactly alike.

At the extreme end of the scale there are those vehicles which bear little similarity to the normal trucks which we see every day. Included in this category should be the fully-tracked types for carrying equipment to very remote areas across wild countryside, or the monster-tracked platforms for transporting space rockets to the launch platform. At the lower end of the scale we have the more mundane little 4 × 4s used the world over for carrying men and equipment to areas off the normal highways. In between these two extremes there are a great many varieties of interest.

The world of the small 4 × 4 has expanded rapidly since World War 2. In pre-war days the 4 × 4 was met with very rarely in civilian operations and even many military vehicles were not so well equipped. The legendary Jeep changed all that. For the twenty or so years following the end of the war many thousands of little Willys or Ford-built runabouts were busy performing a wide variety of tasks for farmers, builders, contractors and the service industries.

Following in the wake of the US Jeep, the British Land-Rover achieved considerable following as a general workhorse for both agriculture and industry. In the early post-war years a high proportion of its sales were assured by virtue of the fact that large numbers were sold to countries within the Commonwealth. More recently, there has been increased competition in this area of the vehicle market from other manufacturers as the demand for light cross-country trucks has increased. In addition to being produced in Britain the Land-Rover is built under licence in several other

1

2

1. *Saviem TP3 4 × 4 operating in the desert.*

2. *Widely sold in pro-Soviet countries is the Belaz 4 × 4 otherwise known as the UAZ 452D. Load is 1 ton.*

3. *Underside view of the Fiat model 65 4 × 4 showing disposition of transfer box and drive axles.*

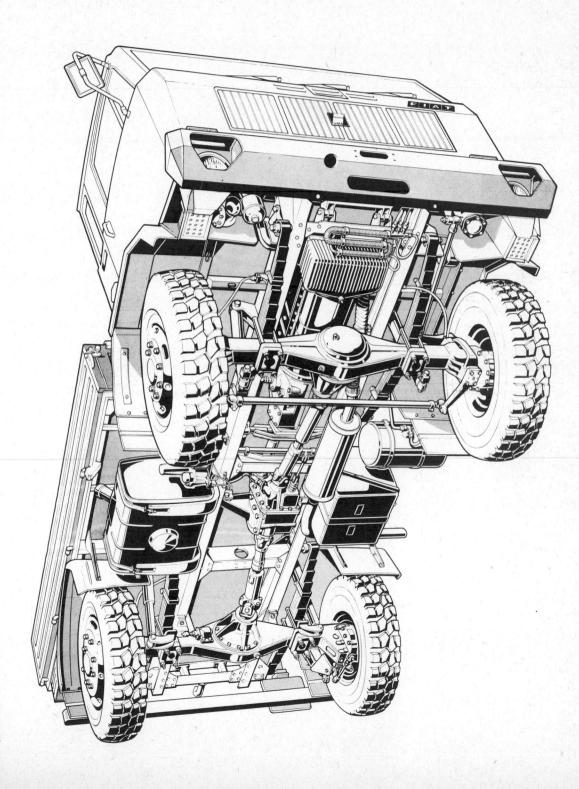

countries, and the American Jeep is also built out-side the USA under similar franchise arrange-ments.

Whereas the Land-Rover still functions as a working vehicle, the Jeep has grown into some-thing quite different. Although goods-carrying types are produced, it is the luxury personnel car-riers with which the Jeep name is associated more readily today. Similarly, the Range Rover has filled a need for a more luxurious 'private' type of vehicle and looks more at home at a ski resort than up to its axles in manure like its more everyday counter-parts.

Another contender for the light 4 × 4 market is the Stonefield, which was first presented to the public in 1976. This is a forward control vehicle, originally offered in four-wheel form but a 6 × 4 version was later introduced. Unlike many other all-wheel-drive vehicles, the Stonefield does not have the conventional ladder type pressed steel frame. It relies instead upon a space frame made up of welded square section steel tubing.

Power is supplied by either V6 or V8 petrol engines, and is then transferred via an automatic transmission to a transfer gearbox which arranges the drive to both axles in the 4 × 4 or the first two axles in the 6 × 4. Suspension is by leaf springs and the two models are rated at 3900 lb and 5030 lb respectively.

The military, as well as fire brigades, public authorities and the service industries, has shown interest in the 4 × 4. In addition, some of the 6 × 4s are in service as camera trucks and motorway emergency vehicles.

The Mercedes Benz Unimog needs little intro-duction to European readers, for in the past thirty years it has become one of the most flexible of workhorses with regard to a wide variety of tasks in the cross-country, construction, municipal, agricultural and service industry spheres. Acquired by Mercedes Benz in 1951, this light/medium category 4 × 4 has achieved considerable success both at home in Germany and in export markets.

In its original form, the Unimog aimed at the dual role of a highway drawbar tractor for handling one or two trailers and an agricultural tractor. In addition to these two major functions, however, it was aimed at covering the municipal and service fields of operation, by virtue of the fact that it could

be readily adapted as a mobile power-house.

The basic idea of a short wheelbase drawbar tractor was not new, for in pre-war Germany there had been deliberate action to help the local trans-port function by allowing young men to drive this category of vehicle; the towing of several trailers was also actively encouraged in order to achieve higher productivity. With the rapid growth of private motor traffic after the war this freedom was curtailed, and so one of the major markets for the tractors was lost. Consequently, several builders opted out.

The Unimog, therefore, has developed along the lines of a 'jack-of-all-trades' type of vehicle because of its myriad of attachments, although it has retained the basic attributes of cross-country ability plus the traction required to handle heavy loads.

The present range embraces models from 4200 to 9000 kg gross, powered by diesel engines from 2404 to 5675 cc, with wheelbases varying between 2.25 and 3.25 m.

To list the Unimog variations would be imposs-ible. It will suffice to say that it has found use in a very wide spectrum of the vehicle market, includ-ing the roles of street sweeper, fire truck, snow plough, bulldozer, digger, hydraulic loader, effluent tanker, ambulance, bucket loader, rail-road shunter and, of course, agricultural tractor.

Of more recent appearance is the range of small Mercedes Benz cross-country vehicles designated in the 230/240/280/300-series and embracing forty different models. Based on two wheelbase lengths and with van, and soft and hard top personnel carrier body styles, the new vehicle embraces Mer-cedes quality linked with the considerable cross-country experience of Steyr-Daimler-Puch from Austria. A choice of four engines is available:

1. Unimog with Schmidt shovel loader attachment.

2. Older style of Unimog with spreader type hopper body which is easily replaced by flat body when vehicle is required for other duties.

1

2

four- or six-cylinder petrol and four- or five-cylinder diesel.

The Japanese have been particularly active in the light 4 × 4 market in the recent past. The Toyota has sold quite well in many markets of the world, and comes in various body styles and wheelbases. Named the Land Cruiser, it is powered by a 3878 cc petrol engine rated at 145 bhp, although a diesel engine is also available in some countries.

Of smaller size is the Daihatsu, which has an overall length of 11 ft 5 in and is powered by a 1587 cc four-cylinder petrol engine rated at 67 bhp. A diesel engine option is available: 2530 cc producing 62 bhp.

Another diminutive product is the Suzuki LJ80 series from a manufacturer far better known for its motor cycles. Powered by a tiny 797 cc overhead camshaft engine which is rated at 41 bhp, the vehicle has a total length of only 10 ft 5 in.

Somewhat larger with regard to engine size is the Nissan Patrol, with a 130 bhp 3956 cc petrol engine. This vehicle follows the established jeep-type layout and has a wheelbase of 7 ft 2.6 in.

Following a rather different line is the Subaru, for this is a normal small pick-up but with four-wheel-drive mechanicals. Power is provided by a 1595 cc petrol engine of the four-cylinder horizontally-opposed type, and the vehicle features independent suspension all round.

The old established firm of Steyr-Puch in Austria introduced their little Haflinger 4 × 4 originally for the Austrian Army; it was so successful that civilian versions soon followed. With a wheelbase of just under 5 ft and an overall length of 9 ft 4 in, the nimble little truck could scale 40 degree slopes and wade through 18 in of water. Power was supplied by a tiny 643 cc flat-twin petrol engine which was rear-mounted. Drive was then taken through a single dry plate clutch and four-speed gearbox to the rear axle and thence by propellor shaft, sited within the central tubular backbone chassis, to the front axle. Independent coil spring suspension was used for the swing half-axles, and the vehicle used 145 × 12 tyres.

Following their success with the Haflinger, Steyr produced another cross-country vehicle, but this time it had a larger capacity and greater power to match. Named the Pinzgauer, this new entrant for the high mobility stakes is available in both 4 × 4 and 6 × 6 forms and is powered by a 2499 cc

Although this Unimog and trailer has obvious military applications, the photograph clearly demonstrates the rough terrain capabilities of such 4 × 4 vehicles.

1

2

four-cylinder in-line engine. As with the earlier model, the Pinzgauer is based on the tubular backbone type chassis with swinging half-axles; the coil spring suspension is used for the 4 × 4 whereas the rear axles of the 6 × 6 are hung on a pair of parabolic leaf springs. As one would expect, the performance is startling, and its climbing ability limited only by the surface climbed. One contemporary road tester said its limits were determined by the courage of the driver, for on a firm surface it would climb a gradient of 100 per cent!

Not all light cross-country vehicles need this kind of tenacity, though, and most have to ascribe to lower limits on their capabilities. Another way of tackling the all-wheel-drive feature is to take an ordinary vehicle and put it in the hands of one of the specialist converters. This might at first appear

3

1. The 4 × 4 versions of light pickups are becoming increasingly popular for site work by supervisors and maintenance staff.

2. With a performance like the proverbial mountain goat, the Austrian-built Steyr Pinzgauer comes in either four or six wheel layout.

3. Conditions such as these demand the use of a rotary cutter and blower type snowplough with all-wheel-drive.

to be a rather long-winded way of tackling the problem, but often the customer wants features contained in a vehicle that is a conventional production-line model except that only the rear wheels are powered. There are a number of firms specializing in this type of work; for example, Reynolds Boughton and Baja in Britain undertake conversion work on otherwise standard vehicles.

Four-wheel drive (or all-wheel drive) is not something which has recently been developed; it is merely that it is more popular today. Many of the old names in the truck-building business were building such vehicles soon after the motor truck began to get on its feet, and some like Latil in France also featured four-wheel steering. Most truck producers do not bother with all-wheel-drive vehicles, for with a low sales figure they serve only to upset production schedules and involve the stocking of non-standard items which may only rarely be called for.

As far back as the 1930s, four-wheel-drive trucks were very expensive pieces of equipment, because of the very nature of their construction. Each vehicle was virtually hand-built to suit the special purpose for which it was intended. Most of the vehicles were of the heavy type and were used in the logging, mining or oil businesses which could stand such high-cost items of equipment. In the United States of America the name of Marmon-Herrington became synonymous with all-wheel-drive vehicles, for this small enterprise had carved its own little niche in the motor industry by building all-terrain vehicles for anyone who cared to pay. Arthur Herrington, however, finally managed to get one of the biggest producers (Ford) to understand that there was a steady market for more medium weight 4 × 4 trucks in the field of construction companies, power line erectors and highway authorities. So, with the low cost trucks from Ford, Herrington was able to offer the benefits of all-wheel drive to a far wider market, and by dint of sheer volume at a lower price than had previously been the case. Another and probably far more important facet of the Herrington enterprise was the experience gained in building all-wheel-drive vehicles in the years leading up to World War 2, for this expertise made the wholesale production of military equipment possible, and the switch from peacetime trucks was made with little loss of production capacity.

DUMP TRUCKS: MAKES AND SPECIFICATIONS

The site dumper or dump truck is merely an extension of the humble wheelbarrow, but it has singularly done more than any other item of construction equipment to speed up the movement of materials and equipment across countless construction sites.

The extreme height when tipped renders articulated outfits very vulnerable to roll-over when operated on site work.

The basic task for a truck hauling aggregates, stones, earth, rocks, minerals or even plain mud requires that such a vehicle will, at some stage of its operational day, drive off the hard surfaced highway and on to the softer conditions of a quarry or construction site. The conditions found 'off-highway' can vary from a hard gravel track to axle-deep mud, and therefore vehicles operating in such conditions are usually specified to cope with such local site conditions and requirements.

Few operators would consider using anything less than a 4 × 2 16-ton gross truck as the basis for a dump truck. Such a truck would have a payload of between 10 and 11 tons, and its short wheelbase would actually make it more suited for back-street manoeuvring than getting to grips with boggy on-site conditions. Compared with the larger 6 × 4 dual drive machines, 4 × 2 configuration trucks, with their single driving axle, are obviously at a severe disadvantage tractionwise. However, the many thousands in service around the world today play their part in transporting construction and raw materials on and off unbeaten tracks.

With the large number of operational 4 × 2 dump trucks, and even some assorted 4 × 4 all-wheel-drive derivatives, the basic design is still mainly that of an on-road vehicle with strict limitations. However, the heavier 6 × 4 twin driving axle truck offers something more of a compromise.

The need to move maybe 15 tons of earth from a construction site or 16 tons of crushed stone from a rock-crushing plant requires a vehicle with a lot more stamina and tractability. The dual driving axles of the normal 6 × 4 dump truck will often have the added luxury of inter-axle diff-locks which give far better traction when the going gets really soft; however, many such trucks are built in varying degrees of off-highway suitability.

Britain is one of the increasing number of European and other nations to allow the legal use of 8 × 4, twin-steering, twin-driving-axle rigid trucks. Such trucks make ideal dump truck chassis, offering both compactness and rigidity of design, which are the optimum requirements for operation across the undulating terrain found on muddy construction sites. In Britain such trucks are allowed legally to gross 30 tons on the public highway, and as they are primarily constructed as on-highway vehicles their off-highway characteristics vary from manufacturer to manufacturer.

Both the 4 × 2 and 6 × 4 on-highway truck-based dumps echo the design characteristics of the 8 × 4 dump trucks in that they are compromise vehicles suited to highway operation with reasonable site tractability, but they have obvious limitations when it comes to really tough working conditions.

In specifying the right truck for the job the operator has to take into account the traction capabilities of the truck, gradability on hills (as many quarries and construction sites have steep exit ramps), and the correct choice of tyres. In constructing the right truck for the job, the vehicle manufacturer has to install the correct choice of suspension, and high engine power output coupled with suitable gearbox and axle ratios. Ground clearance is of great importance in a vehicle working off-highway, and all too many on/off-highway

Early design of articulated dump truck showing the combined hydraulic/wire-rope system of raising the body. Tipping angle is low compared with later types.

dump trucks have a front axle beam which is too low and which acts like a bulldozer blade when driving across deep mud. This must seriously affect both the truck's steering and required traction effort.

Even exhaust systems have to be carefully routed out of harm's way; and yet there are still a handful of truck builders that take the easy way out and instal the exhaust box either low under the chassis or, even worse, right at the front of the truck under the bumper. A front installation can easily require that the exhaust doubles as a dozer blade; this makes it very susceptible to damage from rocks, mud and water.

The truck manufacturers that have been most successful in the on/off-highway field are those who have incorporated the maximum off-road features into their products. The West German

1

2

3

company Magirus Deutz have become European market leaders in this field, by offering premium quality vehicles which have exceptional go-anywhere capabilities. Having gained much useful experience from building top-selling 6 × 4 and 6 × 6 off-highway dump trucks, Magirus now offer the complete off-road bogie on the 8 × 4 dump truck chassis. This in itself has a specially designed flexing chassis, which gives the greatest amount of axle movement and flotation essential to retain traction in the deepest mud.

In certain cases articulated or tractor/semi-trailer rigs are required for use as dump trucks. Obviously, within the length laws of any country, semi-trailer combinations can be much longer than any rigid truck; however, with quarry and construction materials being very much dead weight, the extra length available is often of little use.

Although not perhaps the ideal choice of vehicle, semi-trailer rigs are often popular with the operator who runs a mixed fleet of both general and tipping trailers. He can thus interchange tractors from long-haul highway traffic to on/off-highway dump trucking, as and when the need arises.

Semi-trailer dump trucks are particularly popu-

1. On this site sets of 'doubles' are quickly handled by two loaders working simultaneously.

2. Mack model A40 dump truck posed alongside a Lorain rope-operated face shovel in 1951.

3. Ex military equipment was pressed into service after World War 2: this London Demolition contractor used many Macks in their fleet.

lar in the Middle East, where the use of large tractors is more acceptable, and these rigs often gross around 65 tons or more.

The very fact that the trailer is coupled to the tractor by the means of a flexible fifth-wheel coupling means that the whole rig is not as rigid as the conventional dump truck, and so the semi-trailer combination has severe limitations off-highway. It is not uncommon for such a rig to overturn its trailer when tipping out a load on uneven ground. With less imposed axle loading than a big dump truck, the tractor usually has less traction capability as well.

Moving away from vehicles which are based on

Scammell 'Mountaineer' 8/10 cubic yard dump truck was used in both home and overseas markets.

normal highway trucks, there are many dump trucks which are designed and engineered specifically as on- and off-highway machines – no compromises, no minor alterations to basic on-road specifications and no prayers are needed to get them through the mud!

Designed with full off-road suspensions, diff-locks, off-road tyres and tough yet flexible chassis, these beasts of burden are as much at home wading through axle-deep mud as they are trundling down the tarmac highway. Although they are limited to 24–26 tonnes' gross weight on European highways, these 6 × 4 trucks are not restricted in gross weight once they leave the public highway and head out across the more arduous 'roads' of quarries, mines and construction sites.

Scania, Volvo, Mercedes, Berliet, Magirus Deutz, Fiat, Mack, MAN, Foden, Kraz and Tatra are just some of the assorted manufacturers from around the world who build dump trucks with good off-highway performance. Although limited to the legal maximum on public roads, most machines are designed to gross out at much higher weights off-road, usually between 30 and 40 tons.

Manufacturers such as the West German Magirus Deutz and the Czechoslovakian Tatra have standardized the use of air-cooled diesel engines for their range of trucks; this completely alleviates the need for radiators, water pumps and the associated hoses and piping, a fault in any of which can often put a normal water-cooled diesel truck out of action. Tatra and Magirus, together with the Austrian OAF company, which also markets its 'Jumbo' trucks under a licence agreement with the German MAN concern, prefer to incorporate the added extra of a driven front steering axle in the specification of their really heavyweight machines.

It is this type of truck, with its compact size, excellent off-road traction capabilities and ability to conform to the tough legislation covering the operation of such a truck on public highways, that

*Russian-built Mogilev 20-ton capacity dump truck
undergoing proving trials.*

is proving very popular around the world today.
From the industrialized areas of Germany to the
barren wastes of the Middle East, from the jungles
of Africa to Russia and even Australia, the same
trucks will be found hauling immense loads on and
off the highway. These are probably some of the
most tortured and abused trucks in the world.

The very fact that different types of raw
materials, rocks, coal, sand and even basic earth,
have varying specific gravities means that no one
standard size of dump body will be able to hold the
same weight capacity for a standard size load.
Therefore many operators will specify a body large
enough to carry the maximum weight of a lightweight substance, and, in theory, the truck body
should only be partially loaded with a heavier substance, in order to avoid a gross overload!

In many of the developing and Third World
countries, overloading on public highways is not
uncommon, nor for that matter is the use for highway operation of large or purely off-highway dump
trucks. With most on/off-highway trucks operated
in the Western world, the truck operator will at
some time or other want to use the truck on a public
highway. In order to comply with the highway
legislation of the land the truck must therefore
conform to certain size and weight (and probably
also braking and lighting) legislation.

It suits many dump truck operators to run trucks
that can load at one off-highway site, truck over the
public highway at a reasonable speed and then
unload at another site across town. Other such
trucks may be used in excess of their legal on-
highway gross weight load when operating purely
off-road, but can be driven empty on the public
highway from job to job as the operator wishes.

For the dump truck operator who has no need
for trucks to be used on the public highway, or who
wishes to haul loads on-site above 40 tonnes gross,
there is a large selection of pure off-highway
machinery. Once into this league of big dump
trucks, most of the names associated with normal

roadgoing trucks are soon forgotten and left far behind; such is the speciality of construction associated with the 'super-heavies'.

In the lower gross weight categories, names such as Kenworth, Foden, Berliet, Faun, Kaelble and Scammell can readily be associated with their roadgoing counterparts, although the resulting vehicles often bear little resemblance to their original namesakes.

In Britain the Foden company has long been associated with building off-highway dump trucks and is now the only British truck manufacturer to build a range of both normal highway and off-road heavyweight machinery.

Foden build a range of chunky two-axle dump trucks with load capacities of up to 20 tons, all of which are Cummins diesel-powered machines. In fact Foden has standardized the installation of Cummins engines throughout its range of off-road dump trucks, using the six-cylinder NTA855 series diesels, ranging from 280 to 380 bhp in vehicles with payloads of above 20 tons.

The largest truck in the Foden dump truck range is the FC35A 6×4 truck, which has an Allison CLBT750 fully automatic gearbox coupled to its 380 bhp Cummins diesel, and has a load capacity of 35 tons.

At one time AEC built a range of off-highway

Some idea of the rough treatment suffered by dump trucks can be gauged from the load on these two trucks.

dump trucks in Britain culminating in the type 690, 10 cubic yard dump truck which was powered by the AEC AV690 192 bhp six-cylinder diesel. Over the years, production has been moved around the British Leyland manufacturing plants, and this truck has become the Aveling Barford AB690 and the Thornycroft LD55 Bush Tractor, and has ended up as the Scammell LD24 powered by the Leyland L12 engine, although soon to be replaced by the new Leyland T43 Landtrain series.

The West German manufacturers Kaelble have, over the years, built dump trucks with capacities of up to 50 tons. More recently, however, they are concentrating on the lighter end of the market with

1

2

3

4

1. Only the tiny cab indicates the overall size of this Euclid articulated dump truck seen being loaded by a massive face shovel.

2. For on/off-highway operation the rigid four-axle chassis is widely used in Britain and to a lesser extent in mainland Europe.

3. Crane Fruehauf were the builders of these bottom discharge dump trailers of 33 cubic yard capacity, which haul gravel in a Dublin quarry.

4. For a short while Atkinson Lorries of Preston produced a range of chassis specially designed for site work.

20,000 to 27,000 kg payload machines. The German company obviously chooses German-built diesels to power these trucks and the Mercedes Benz OM403 V10-cylinder, 352 bhp engine is featured throughout the range. The other West German manufacturer of heavy dump trucks is Faun, who build a far wider and heavier range of off-highway dump trucks, ranging from 19 to 80 tons' payload. Faun use Deutz air-cooled V-form diesels in their lighter machines, but switch to V12 Cummins and V12 and V16 Detroit Diesel engines for the real heavyweight machinery.

The design, construction and marketing problems of such specialized machinery as off-highway dump trucks are such that over recent years there has been much unrest within the manufacturing industry, with some famous names pulling out of the market, others changing ownership and new companies springing up overnight. Names such as Perlini, Kockums, Komatsu, Euclid, Terex, Lec-trahaul, Wabco and Caterpillar may be unfamiliar to those outside the industry, for such is the speciality of manufacturing and building techniques involved in producing a truly off-highway

Largest dump truck in the world is the Terex Titan at present operating in British Columbia.

dump truck that few of these monster trucks are seen outside their natural environment.

It is perhaps hard to imagine a 4 × 2 truck having a payload of 100 tons or more, but then these are no ordinary trucks. These dump trucks are built from the ground up to undertake a very specialized task, and, with no size or weight limitations to restrict the designers, they often dwarf all around, including roadgoing trucks and even buildings

Brute power is one basic rule of thumb, and whereas an on-road tractor-trailer rig needs around 250–300 bhp to haul around 30–35 tons' gross weight at speed along a smooth tarmac highway a great deal more is needed to haul maybe 85 tons of rock on the back of a large dump truck over undulating dirt tracks. Most 85-ton capacity dump trucks, for instance, have diesels with power outputs of between 800 and 870 bhp, and this rela-

*Pair of Terex model R45 dump trucks being
transported to a site on low loaders because of their
non-compliance with road-going vehicle legislation.*

tively high output is often in excess of the bhp per
ton figure associated with highway trucks.

Normal leaf spring suspensions are not too popular on trucks operating above 40 tons gross,
because they are unable to stand up to the constant
pounding encountered on unmade roads. Many
manufacturers use huge coil springs on trucks with
payloads of up to 30 tons; however, above this
weight the wide use of rubber, hydraulic and
pneumatic suspensions takes over. Some manufacturers use sandwich rubber units loaded in compression. Others use ride cylinders containing
energy-absorbing silicone fluids, and although
these give a necessary hard and rigid ride much
driver pounding is eliminated by the fitting of a
good suspension seat.

Obviously everything about monster dump
trucks is of a heavyweight and robust nature, and

this especially includes the drive-line set-up. With
such high gross weights, and the monstrous engine
horsepower and torque produced, a clutch and
manual gearbox arrangement is unthinkable.
There does not exist a manual gearbox that could
handle the massive torque being thrown out by an
870 bhp Caterpillar engine and the size of the
clutch plate needed to transfer the power does not
bear thinking about.

Whereas some manufacturers install manual
gearboxes in trucks around the 20-ton class, most
mid-range vehicles are fitted with automatic gearboxes. The now discontinued Mack M75SX 75-ton
capacity dump truck had an autogearbox, as do the
heavier Caterpillar 777 85-tonner, the Euclid R105
105-ton capacity machine and also the really heavy
Terex 33–14 series 130-ton payload truck, which is
powered by a massive 1350 bhp turbocharged and
inter-cooled diesel.

However, these same automatic gearboxes have
strict limitations with a useful application of up to
around 150 tons' capacity. At this upper weight
limit the usefulness of automatic gearboxes, prop-
shafts and conventional axle and drive-line set-ups

as we know them is severely limited, because of the sheer size and power output from the engines needed to motivate such huge trucks.

Instead, electric motors take over where conventional gearboxes leave off, and the resulting system is similar to that used in diesel-electric railroad locomotives. Wabco, Terex, Euclid and Lectrahaul are all firm users of electric drive systems in their big trucks. The basic idea for the drive system uses the diesel engine to turn a chassis-mounted electric generator. The electric generator in turn provides current which powers huge electric motors installed in the wheel assemblies, thus providing very powerful and ultra-smooth traction

which is essential when motivating maybe 300 tons of dump truck on stop/start work.

As stated before, these monster trucks use very high power output diesels, and this severely limits the manufacturer's actual choice in power units. Although the world-wide market in diesels around the 200–300 bhp category may be fierce and competitive, once above 500 bhp the choice thins out alarmingly. Both Cummins and Detroit Diesel engines feature almost exclusively in this high horsepower engine market, with DD engines taking the lion's share.

Although Caterpillar trucks use their own 'Cat' diesels throughout their product range, their

The articulated dump truck with bottom discharge is often preferred for use when controlled unloading over a wide area is necessary.

largest engine is the V12 D348, which churns out some 870 bhp at the flywheel. The Cummins V12 VTA 1710C 655 bhp engine features heavily in trucks with payloads of up to 75 tons, but above this figure the engine market is almost exclusively dominated by Detroit Diesel and General Motors EMD.

Detroit Diesel actually sell approximately 60 per cent of their engine output to the off-highway truck market. The 149 series engines were designed almost exclusively for construction and mining vehicle applications, and can today be found operating in many countries, including Zambia, Peru and China.

Whereas naturally-aspirated and turbocharged versions of the 12V71 and 16V71 series engines can be found in lower weight machines, once above 100 tons' payload the really big engines take over. The Euclid R120 120-ton capacity dump truck features the DD 12V-149TI rated at 1200 bhp, and this same power plant is also featured in the Wabco 120C, although a Cummins KTA 2300 rated at 1200 bhp can also be specified for the Wabco.

The largest Detroit Diesel is the 16V-149 TI which produces some 1600 bhp, and this can be found in the Wabco 170 CW and the Terex 3315B, both 170-ton capacity vehicles. There are only three dump trucks which can haul loads above this

payload figure; they are constructed by Wabco, Lectrahaul and Terex and must surely rank as the biggest trucks in the world.

The Wabco Haulpak 3200B is a 6 × 4 truck with a payload capacity of up to 235 tons and a body capacity of some 210 cubic yards. Power for this impressive beast comes from a General Motors EMD Railroad locomotive diesel engine which produces some 2475 bhp at just 900 rpm, and this is in turn coupled to a General Motors electric generator and motor drive system. The truck is brought to rest by 3150 hp capacity electric dynamic retardation, caused by converting the wheel drive motors into generators, thus producing a braking effect. Some fifty Wabco Haulpak

Kenworth model 548 6×4 coal hauler. The large capacity Union tipping body is heated by the exhaust as with most dump trucks.

3200Bs are now in service around the world, although most are in the open-cast mines of America, Canada and Australia. Once termed the 'Giant of Trucks', the Wabco has recently been dwarfed by a newcomer to the scene: the Terex Titan.

Officially known as the Terex 33–19, the Titan quite modestly claims to be the largest truck in the world to carry a load on its back. The Titan was built in answer to the growing requirements of mine operators around the world for machines to transport ever increasing amounts of earth, coal, rock and ore. The specification of the Titan is quite impressive: the truck is 66 feet long, 25 feet wide and 22 feet high from the ground to the top of the canopy over the cab; however, with the body raised, its overall height increases to 56 feet.

Once again a General Motors EMD Railroad locomotive diesel engine powers this big truck – a V16 EMD 16–645E4 unit. This engine produces a gross figure of 3300 hp (2462 kW) at just 900 rpm, with some 3000 hp (2238 kW) being delivered at the flywheel. The 16-ton engine is coupled to the usual electric drive system which transfers the power to the road by way of ten huge 40.00 × 57.60 tyres, each of which weighs just over $3\frac{1}{2}$ tons.

With a maximum heaped capacity body of 287 cubic yards, the Terex Titan has a load capacity of an unbelievable 317,520 kg (350 short tons) giving the truck a total gross weight of 553,573 kg (610 short tons).

Despite its gargantuan proportions, the Terex Titan can still power its way up to 30 mph on site; but what about the problem of getting the 33–19 Titan from site to site? It obviously cannot travel under its own power over the public highway, as its width alone would take up at least two lanes of any highway, and both size and weight would present quite a problem for any heavy hauling company attempting to carry it on a trailer. The Titan is therefore broken down into its component parts and shipped on eight railroad trucks to the nearest point of destination, where the truck is re-assembled. Erection of the Titan requires some 400–600 man-hours to assemble the complete vehicle, depending on the exact facilities, people and equipment available at site. The specialized equipment needed includes two mobile cranes, 1 × 75-ton and 1 × 100-ton capacity, a fork-lift truck, welding equipment and air compressors.

SPECIFICATIONS

HAULAMATIC 620 Mk 2.

Manufactured by:	Haulamatic Ltd, Heanor, Derbyshire.
Engine:	Perkins V8.640 developing 160 kw or Caterpillar V8.3208 öf 167 kw.
Transmission:	Allison automatic with five forward ratios.
Drive:	6×4.
Tyres:	Front 12.00×20, rear 16.00×20.
General:	Payload of 20,000 kg, gross weight 30,800 kg.

D.J.B. D550

Manufactured by:	D.J.B. Engineering Ltd, Peterlee, Co. Durham
Engine:	Caterpillar 3408PCTA 8-cylinder producing 328 kw. Turbocharged and aftercooled.
Transmission:	Caterpillar 988B powershift with four forward speeds.
Drive:	6×4 (front and first axle of bogie).
Tyres:	33.25×29 radials.
General:	Rated load 50 tonnes, gross weight 87.1 tonnes.

AVELING–BARFORD CENTAUR 40

Manufactured by:	Aveling–Barford Ltd, Grantham.
Engine:	Caterpillar 1693TA 6-cylinder turbocharged and aftercooled producing 425 bhp or GM Detroit Diesel 12V–71 two-stroke producing 476 bhp.
Transmission:	Six speed manual gearbox with the Caterpillar engine or Allison Torqmatic six speed with either engine.
Drive:	4×2
Tyres:	18.00×33
General:	Payload 36,287 kg, gross weight 64,591 kg

PERLINI T.20

Manufactured by:	Roberto Perlini, S. Bonifacio, Verona.
Engine:	GM Detroit Diesel 6V–71N producing 265 bhp.
Transmission:	ZF six speed manual
Drive:	4×2
Tyres:	14.00×24
General:	Payload 20,000 kg, gross weight 34,500 kg

CATERPILLAR 773 rear end dump truck

Manufactured by:	Caterpillar Tractor Co, USA.
Engine:	Caterpillar D346 V8 cylinder diesel developing 600 bhp at 1900 rpm.
Transmission:	9-speed Caterpillar powershift automatic.
Drive:	4 × 2.
Tyres;	2100 × 35.
General:	The Cat 773 has a load capacity of 50 tons (US) or 45.4 t and weighs 37,200 kg empty. Oil-cooled disc brakes are fitted to the rear wheels.

HEATHFIELD H20 dump truck

Manufactured by:	Heathfield Engineering Ltd, Newton Abbot, England.
Engine:	British Leyland UE680 series diesel, naturally aspirated 6-cylinder engine, developing 200 bhp at 2200 rpm. ** Optional engine is the Rolls Royce CE220 diesel.
Transmission:	Fuller T905F gearbox giving 5 forward speeds and 1 reverse. ** The Fuller T905J gearbox is fitted to the Rolls Royce engine.
Drive:	4 × 2.
Front axle:	Heathfield design.
Rear axle:	Heathfield planetary hub reduction type.
Tyres:	1400 × 25 rock pattern.
General:	This off-highway truck has a payload of 18,200 kg.

KAELBLE K 20B rear dump truck

Manufactured by:	Carl Kaelble GMBH, Backnang, West Germany.
Engine:	Mercedes Benz OM 355 6-cylinder diesel developing 265 bhp at 2200 rpm.
Transmission:	ZF 6-speed synchromesh.
Drive:	4 × 2.
Front axle:	Kaelble design.
Rear axle:	Kaelble design.
Tyres:	1400 × 24.
General:	Unladen weight – 15,100 kg. Payload – 20,000 kg. Gross weight – 35,000 kg.

MACK R897RSX

Manufactured by:	Mack Trucks, Brisbane, Australia.
Engine:	Mack V8 ENDT 866 375 bhp diesel.
Transmission:	CL75 clutch and 12-speed air-shift.
Drive:	8 × 4.
Rear axles:	Mack SWD69 80,000-lb capacity bogie.
Tyres:	Michelin 1400 × 24.
General:	Three units currently operating at Shay Gap ore mine.

FODEN Superhaulmaster 6 × 4 rigid, type RC29/26

Manufactured by:	Foden Ltd, Sandbach, England.
Engine:	Cummins Formula E290 6-cylinder diesel rated at 290 bhp at 1900 rpm.
Transmission:	Foden 8-speed gearbox.
Front axle:	Foden.
Rear axles:	Foden build featuring diff-locks and two-spring rear bogie.
General:	This left-hand drive export model can gross up to 26,000 kg.

TATRA 813 series heavy duty truck

Manufactured by:	Tatra Motors, Praha, Czechoslovakia.
Engine:	Tatra 930–31 diesel rated at 270 bhp. V12 cylinder engine featuring air-cooling.
Transmission:	Tatra 5-speed.
Chassis:	Tatra is unique in that it features an unusual central spine chassis with swing half-axles.
Drive:	All-wheel drive 8 × 8.
Tyres:	18 × 22.5.
General:	With the relatively high kerb weight of some 12,700 kg for the unbodied chassis, the Tatra 813 can gross out at 36,000 kg.

KENWORTH 548 series coal hauler

Engine:	Cummins KT 450 rated at 450 bhp (sae) at 2100 rpm.
Transmission:	Allison CLBT 750 Automatic with retarder.
Front axle:	Rockwell FU910 28,000 lb capacity.
Rear axles:	Rockwell SR 570 Planetary Reduction, 120,000 lb capacity. Inter-axle differential lock-out.
Tyres:	1600 × 25. 24-ply tubeless.
General:	Load capacity 50 short tons in 22 foot long body, 12 foot wide.

AIRCRAFT SERVICING VEHICLES

Although not strictly off-highway vehicles, the items of equipment used to service the commercial aircraft in use today are of interest, if only because they are so rarely seen outside their working environment and some are prohibited from using normal roads because of size or weight restrictions.

High tractive effort combined with low overall height are prime factors in the design of aircraft towing tractors.

The needs of aircraft servicing have led to the production of some rather unusual vehicles in recent years. As modern aircraft have become of larger capacity and more numerous (and more expensive!), there have been demands for vehicles to carry out a variety of highly-specialized tasks with the minimum of delay.

The initial movement of aircraft within the confines of the servicing areas, aprons and repair bays is by tug. These special vehicles are designed within parameters concerning power, manoeuvreability and low height. A modern high-capacity airliner such as the Boeing 747 weighs 562,000 lb (710,000 lb fully loaded), requiring a towing vehicle of ample power, although unlike a roadgoing vehicle the aircraft tug operates on a level surface. In addition to having sufficient power it is important that the tug has adequate traction, especially when starting from rest. In order to achieve this feature, the vehicle has large-diameter wheels with tyres of ample section, either limited suspension or none at all, and a low maximum speed but a considerable tractive effort. To obtain adequate adhesion, the tractor has to be of substantial construction and weight, and fitted with a torque converter and direct drive, or perhaps a two-speed automatic gearbox if a high road speed is required for empty running between towing jobs.

The towing vehicles are necessarily of low height for ease of movement around parked aircraft, and the driver is positioned low down where he has a good view of the towbar coupling to the aircraft. Often the aircraft tugs are completely open in order to retain low profile as well as maintaining a good view for the driver, although recent trends are toward a proper cab for safety and comfort.

Having moved the aircraft into position on the apron or servicing area by the use of one of the tugs, it will then be the turn of the aircraft fueller to refill the aircraft fuel tanks in readiness for the flight. This has to be carried out before any passengers are allowed on to the aircraft, in the interests of safety.

As with the fuelling of vintage motor-cars, early aircraft were supplied with fuel by means of the ubiquitous 2-gallon can, until the 1920s when the first bulk tankers came into use. The fuel was transferred from tanker to aircraft by a hand pump fitted to the tanker. Later developments have included powered pumps to transfer the load, calibrating equipment to measure the amount

Early design of Thompson Brothers aircraft lubricating unit which features a three wheel layout and incorporates Ford engine and running units.

Period picture showing the integral design of aircraft fueller built by Thompson Brothers in the period following World War 2. Leyland engine and axles are used in the design.

transferred, and more recently the exclusion of tankers from the airfield by the provision of underground fuel supply pipes with dispensers sited at strategic points. This has resulted in vehicles for aircraft fuelling merely carrying out pumping and calibrating roles. The fuel supply pipe system, however, is a very recent development, with merely a handful of airfields being so equipped. By far the majority of airports still retain the established mobile fuel tankers for the fuelling of aircraft, and several manufacturers still specialize in this type of equipment.

Basically, the aircraft fueller is a tanker not dissimilar to those used for the normal transport of liquid fuels from oil terminal to customer. They are, however, made much more complex by the additional equipment necessary for their purpose (which involves far more than the delivery of say 10,000 litres of petrol to a filling station, in which case their role would be more or less similar to a pipeline). On the airfield, these vehicles not only transport the fuel from the storage vessel to the aircraft but they also have to measure accurately the amount delivered; this is important, even if only for invoicing!

Additionally, the fuel is carefully filtered, for dirty fuel at 30,000 ft can be hazardous. The vehicle is also fitted with powerful pumping equipment in order to lift the fuel into the tanks of the aircraft, and this needs to be carried out with a minimum of delay, for aircraft terminal delays are expensive, and during the height of the holiday season space is also at a premium. Another feature of these vehicles is the provision of a working platform so that the operative can safely couple the fuel hoses to the aircraft fuel tanks.

All these important aspects have to be brought together in the one vehicle, and in recent years the designers were given another headache with the demand that these fuellers should be capable of fuelling aircraft from beneath the wings, and not alongside as was previously the case. This meant that the huge tanker designs of the 1950s and 1960s were no longer acceptable and the future lay in

fuellers which were no higher than 100 in (2.54 m). This might seem reasonable, for aircraft aprons are alive with all types of servicing vehicles and equipment, and to locate the fueller under the wings means that it does not interfere with water tankers, generators, baggage trucks, refreshment vans and so on.

This location of the tanker also means that a shorter pipe run is required from fueller to aircraft fuel tank, bearing in mind that the fuel tanks are in the wings. In order to reduce the risk of ruptured fuel pipes there have been trials with rigid pipes direct from fueller to aircraft, but this requires great precision in positioning of the fueller below the aircraft filler as well as problems arising with the weight transference as loading proceeds. Nevertheless, the lowering of aircraft fuellers by almost half to obtain the required under-wing positioning brought two problems in its wake – either the new generation of fuellers would be of less capacity, if they were to remain within reasonable overall length, or, if the large capacity was to

be retained, then a very long vehicle would be the result. Mention has already been made of the fact that the servicing area around aircraft is already cramped as all and sundry try to get the aircraft 'turned round' in the allotted time. Therefore any fueller that is over-length will create even more pressure on the space available for the servicing vehicles.

Many fuel companies resort to the use of trailers to attain a high capacity, while still providing a vehicle which is not too unwieldy; for, although an airport first appears almost limitless in size, it soon becomes apparent that at busy times there is considerable pressure on the space adjacent to the loading areas. Not only do airline operators demand quick turn-rounds on their aircraft, but the increasing use of larger aircraft also means that fuel capacities are greater, requiring therefore the use of larger diameter pipes and more powerful pumps in order to ensure a speedy refuel. Some idea of the progress which has been made in this direction is provided by comparing the 1.5 in bore

The low overall height of this Struver aircraft fueller is apparent in this side view. Operator's platform and hosereel are located at the extreme rear.

pipe of a 1948 fueller delivering 85 gallons a minute with the output of 1000 gallons a minute delivered through the 4 in hose used on some hydrant type dispensers. These hydrant dispenser vehicles are not, strictly speaking, aircraft fuellers in the usually accepted sense, for they have no fuel-carrying facility and are basically a mobile pumping/calibrating unit which acts as a dispenser between fuel hydrant point and aircraft.

Another point which emphasizes the increasing sophistication of the modern fueller is that relating to manning of the vehicles and safety of the operatives. In the early post-war years, fueller equipment included a free-standing ladder for reaching the fuel tank, whereas today's equipment embraces a built-in hydraulic platform complete with hoses to hand, and a guard rail.

Safety is one aspect of aircraft fuelling which demands constant vigilance, and it is the major factor which influences the design and manufacture of fuellers world-wide. The amount of fuel carried and dispensed by fuellers has increased enormously over the past few years. Not so long ago 2000 gallons was sufficient to refuel an aircraft used on intercontinental flights, but today's fuellers include vehicles capable of carrying 20,000 gallons. Fortunately, one aspect of modern aircraft has helped with regard to safety – the widespread use of kerosene as the fuel for jet engines has resulted in a lessening of fire risk compared with high-octane aviation fuel as used in the old piston-engined planes.

Around the world there are many companies producing road tankers for the normal delivery of fuel oils, petrol, liquefied gas and other petroleum products. The production of aviation fuellers is not quite so simple; for this reason there are fewer firms engaged in the work.

In West Germany the firm of Ad Struver KG have acquired a reputation for their high-quality aircraft fuellers which have been supplied to many oil companies both at home and in export markets. Naturally, with such a wide variety of aircraft to be fuelled, the capacity of fuellers depends to a large extent on the size and number of aircraft using a particular airfield. For the smaller-demand airfields, a fueller of around 10,000 litres' capacity might well be adequate, particularly where only one type of fuel is provided. Where there is a fluctuating demand, a trailer tank could be brought into use when required. This trailer might well be of similar capacity to the fueller, and arrangements could be made for its load to be dispensed through the pump and metering equipment of the towing vehicle.

As mentioned earlier the pressures on space around an aircraft during its short (one hopes) stay on the ground between flights, gave rise to the provision of fuellers which were limited in height to 100 in (2.54 m) so that they could pass and stand beneath the wings of many aircraft.

This unfortunately caused another problem to arise, that of fire hazards should any drops of fuel fall on to the engine compartment of the vehicle parked below. For this reason it was decided that the operator's platform should be mounted at the extreme rear of the vehicle so that the engine compartment was well out in the open and away from danger.

The operator's platform is entered by way of a short ground ladder and then extended by hydraulic means to a convenient position just below the wing of the aircraft being fuelled. Naturally, the operative has to make the connections by hand, for it is impossible to position the fueller with such precision as is required to enable an automatic coupling to be made. Short lengths of flexible hose are used for transferring the fuel from tanker to aircraft wing tank. Even with the hydraulic platform, which is raised vertically, a certain precision is needed by the driver positioning the fueller, for he is situated some 50 or 60 feet away. One design used a hydraulic boom for the operator, which is much more flexible.

In the old designs, where the fuel loading pump was located at the front of the fueller, the provision of a power take-off from the vehicle engine was a comparatively simple matter. With the transfer of

1. Joint Foden/Gloster Saro design for a medium capacity low profile fueller on a rigid chassis.

2. The 100-inch overall height demanded by underwing fuelling is easier to achieve when a frameless trailer tank is used.

1

2

the pumping equipment to the rear of the tanker, the use of a mechanical drive was ruled out and a hydraulic drive system had to be designed.

The very largest of the fuellers in use are those which are used to refuel the wide-bodied jets used on the long intercontinental hauls, particularly the busy transatlantic routes. Taking a transatlantic Boeing 747 as an example, it has been found that something in the order of 125,000 litres of fuel are required to fill the aircraft ready for its return trip. This has meant that even with the new, larger capacity fuellers of capacities in the 65,000 to 80,000 litre bracket it takes two fuellers to refill the aircraft.

In practice it has been found that these high-capacity fuellers have been worthwhile for fuelling a range of other aircraft with smaller fuel capacities, for in some instances one fueller has been able to take the place of two smaller ones. This has the advantage of reducing the fuelling time, because the tanker does not have to make a return trip to the fuel depot to reload. Alternatively, it can service two aircraft in succession. It also leads to less congestion on the apron. To be fair this does have a slight disadvantage in some cases because the larger vehicles are rather unwieldy in tight situations.

To enable the larger fuellers to maintain the flexibility necessary to be able to fuel a variety of aircraft, it has been expedient to equip them with additional delivery hoses of smaller diameter and throughput than those originally called for when dealing with the larger aircraft. This has usually taken the form of arranging short runs of 2.5 in hose and couplings from hosereels of about 40 yds in length, these being in addition to the main outlets mounted on the hydraulic platform.

In the past few years Struver KG of Hamburg have produced an individual type of aircraft fueller which incorporates some interesting innovations. Finding that they were often presented with almost a *fait accompli* by installing their fuelling equipment on a proprietary chassis, they set about designing a complete vehicle from their own viewpoint, namely aircraft fuelling.

The resulting vehicle is of the chassisless variety on the lines of their range of self-supporting semi-trailer designs. It is supported by axles positioned strategically to accept the all-up weight, but the cab, engine, dispenser, pump and loading sections were seen as separate units which could be arranged to suit the particular requirements of the customer. In order to achieve this degree of flexibility, hydrostatic drive is used so that the power unit can be remote from the driven axles, hosereel, pump and operator's platform.

Somewhat similar fuellers have previously been built both in Britain and the USA, although they did not employ the hydrostatic drive concept but relied instead on the more orthodox drive-line arrangements. The British design was by John Thompson and used a rear-mounted Leyland engine arranged transversely, as had been adopted by that maker's Atlantean type bus chassis. This vehicle did, however, employ the monocoque construction method successfully used by Thompsons on earlier vehicles, which again used Leyland running units for both the Tyne eight-wheeled model and the Tweed, which was a twin-steering six-wheeler.

In the United States both White and KW-Dart produced a low height fueller for under-wing operation, relying on Hendrickson rubber suspension for both driven and steering axles.

Early designs of fuellers used a steel tank, which was sometimes aluminium-lined to guard against corrosion. With the later perfection of argon arc welding, the tank builder has been able to fabricate fuellers wholly of aluminium. This has meant less risk of corrosion and impurities in the fuel. Of possibly greater benefit has been the resulting reduction in weight for a tank of given size; added to this is the chassisless concept which allows greater flexibility in design. By strengthening the tank itself in the areas of highest stress, such as where the axles or the tractor coupling is mounted, it has been possible to fabricate a strong vessel. With no chassis frame below the tank it is possible to lower the overall height of the vehicle. By using the maximum section shape of tank – something between a rectangle and an ellipse – and by providing a slightly dropped centre section, the tank contains the maximum capacity within the overall design factors of strength and safety. The form of construction with a wedge-shaped bottom acts as an aid to efficient draining of the load as well as rendering possible the complete draining of any water.

Another problem which arises with the fuelling of aircraft is an arrangement for unloading fuel from an aircraft before it is taken out of service or if the fuel has become contaminated in some way. In addition, the pump pressure used to load the fuel should be free from sudden surges which could cause a hose to burst. In cases where two fuellers are both engaged in fuelling one aircraft, working pressures should be similar; otherwise the more powerful pump could well be pushing fuel through the aircraft's tanks and back into the second tanker! Naturally, the tanks contained in the wings of the aircraft are connected so that during flight a balance is retained in both wings. This facility could have dire consequences during loading if the fueller were to pump fuel so quickly that the majority of the load entered one wing tank first, so upsetting the balance of the aircraft.

Safety plays a great part in the design and operation of such sophisticated and vulnerable pieces of equipment. Luckily, modern jet fuel is nowhere near as volatile as the high-octane aviation spirits used on the older piston-engined aircraft, but this does not mean that it can be 'slopped' about with gay abandon. The use of radio contact is important to ensure a swift response from the airport fire brigade in an emergency, for the fueller carries only the minimal number of fire extinguishers. All vehicle wiring is fully insulated and the fueller itself must be well earthed before unloading commences. Other safety features include the 'dead man' type of control for the flow of fuel, which demands the attention of the operative for the whole time the fuel is being pumped, and a lock on the vehicle brake system which prevents the vehicle from being driven away until all the hoses have been disconnected and safely stowed away.

As the fuel capacity of large aircraft is so great and the number in use is gradually expanding, so the demand for rapid fuelling and a quicker turn-round is made more apparent. On some large airfields the installation of hydrant systems means that a much smaller fuelling vehicle is used, with resultant easing of congestion around aircraft on the apron. The hydrant system does away with the aircraft fueller as such, for the fuel is piped direct from the remote fuel storage tanks to a hydrant positioned somewhere adjacent to the parked aircraft. A hydrant dispenser vehicle is used to provide the pumping, filtration, calibration and bridging functions between the hydrant and the aircraft itself. With no large fuel supply to carry, the hy-

drant dispenser vehicle is built on much smaller lines than that of the conventional fueller, so saving on cost and space while leading to much easier manoeuvreability. Even with the largest of aircraft the fuel loading can take place from one standpoint, and there is considerable saving on time because there is no fuel tanker to load in the first place.

Drawbacks to the hydrant system are also unfortunately considerable. The initial cost of installation is high and extensions to the system once installed may involve work across the actual runways, unless the work goes hand in hand with overall extensions to the airport facilities themselves.

Another problem arises with airport hydrant systems which, because of cost, are shared between different oil companies. This arrangement may lead to friction with regard to priorities over aircraft fuelling at peak times. There is also the problem encountered when an aircraft needs to be 'defuelled' or unloaded prior to it being taken out of service for some reason or another. At peak times of operation there may be a queue of aircraft waiting to be fuelled which just cannot be handled by the fixed hydrant system. In cases such as these, the use of mobile fuellers is necessary to maintain the necessary flexibility of operation.

Therefore, with such a large number of variables, it is not surprising to find that hydrant systems are not as widespread as one might think, and the aircraft fueller manufacturers continue to strive to produce equipment capable of meeting the exacting requirements of the airline operators, airport authorities and oil companies.

The loading of stores, luggage or freight into an aircraft requires some means of lifting the packages from the vehicle up to the doorway of the aircraft. With many of the older and smaller types of planes, which parked on the main undercarriage wheels and the tail, the loading doors were not far off the ground and there was little problem in transferring the freight. But with the modern designs of aircraft which have a fuselage which remains horizontal, because they stand on a nose wheel in addition to the main undercarriage, the loading hatch is some 3 or 4 metres off the ground.

For the purpose of loading these aircraft, special vehicles have been produced. Their design includes hydraulic rams which lift the complete

*Both hydrant dispenser and bulk fueller types
alongside a Concorde.*

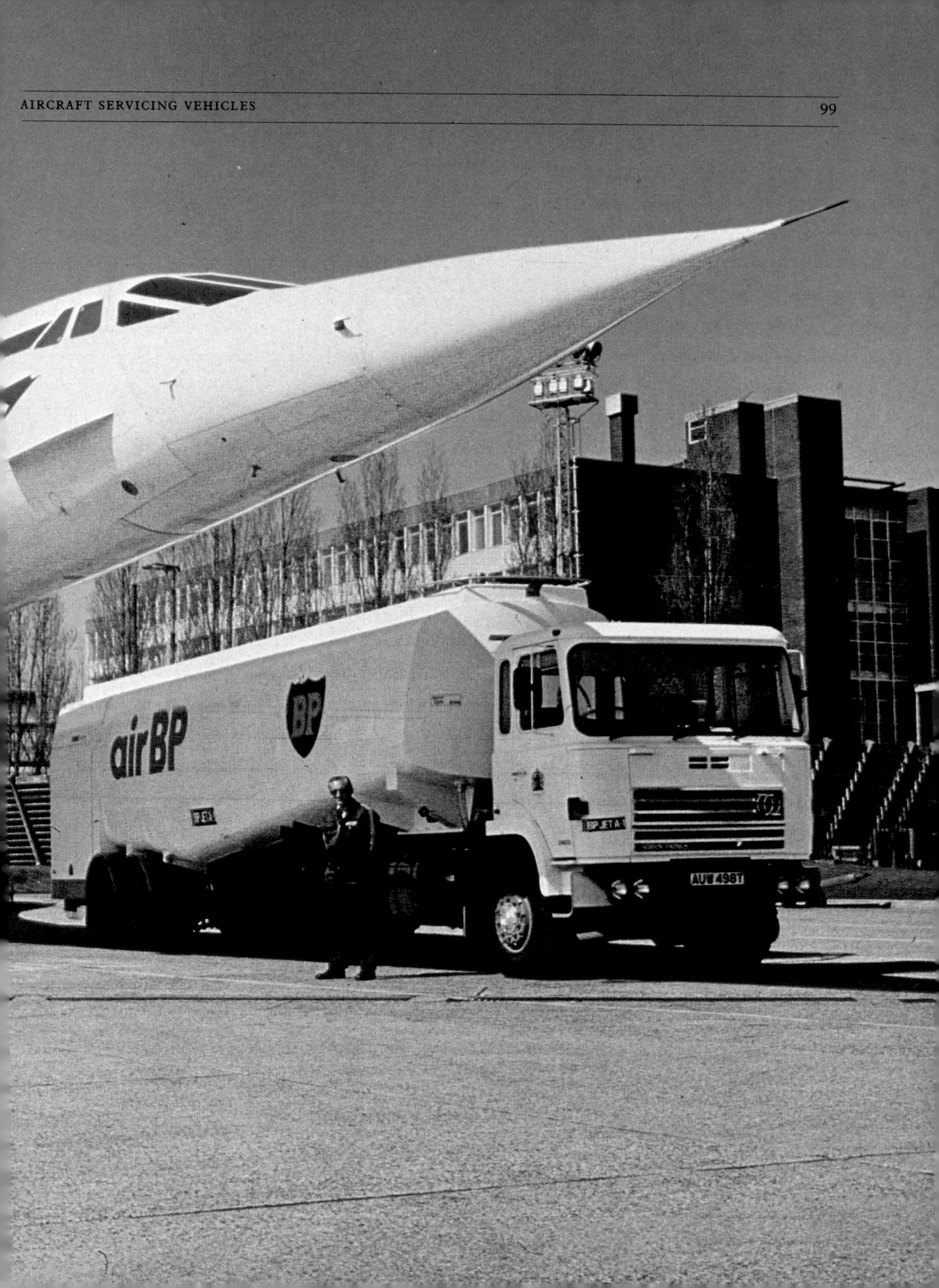
air BP
BP
BP JET A-1
AUW 498T

1

1. *Keeping the vast space of an airport clear of snow is a formidable task, often requiring the use of several machines.*

2 and 3. *Ford D Series with Edbro scissor type elevating equipment for Swissair cargo loader seen in the elevated and closed positions. Loading height is variable for different aircraft.*

2 3

body and its load up to the height of the aircraft loading doors. Some of these vehicles are, in fact, normal roadgoing trucks adapted by means of fitting hydraulic rams and stabilizers, but there are others which remain within the confines of the airport and consist of a mobile loading platform. These latter vehicles often have special cargo handling attachments built into their design so that quite large and heavy pallets can be handled expeditiously. One such design has a load platform consisting of several hundred rollers or wheels so that the pallet can be manhandled with ease. A similar system is adopted within the aircraft itself, in the warehouse and on the transport vehicles. In order that any loads shall be within the loading space of the aircraft fuselage, a system of closed pallets is in use, these having a contour similar to the upper half of the aircraft cargo space.

Other special vehicles seldom seen outside the airport include fresh water dispensers, de-icing equipment, hydraulic platforms, mobile cranes, snow ploughs, foam-laying tankers, aircraft crash tenders, aircraft starters and in more recent times security vehicles.

In many instances the vehicles have much in common with normal trucks and differ only in respect of the equipment carried, whereas others embody special features necessary for them to carry out their particular duty. The water dispenser, therefore, is merely a water tanker with a pump for refilling the aircraft storage tank. An aircraft starter would be a normal truck chassis, fitted with a separate powerful engine and the ancillary equipment required to start the engines of the aircraft.

A runway foam tanker, on the other hand, might well be a high-capacity road tanker equipped with wide booms on which are carried a series of nozzles to spray a wide strip of the runway with foam. In the event of an emergency, such as the arrival of an aircraft which has problems with its undercarriage, leaking fuel or other malfunction which may give rise to danger upon landing, these foam spreaders are called out to lay a foam carpet.

The aircraft crash tenders are rather special, in that modern airliners carry large quantities of fuel and a great many passengers, and any emergencies require a formidable amount of equipment which can traverse the airfield at a rapid pace. For this purpose a larger than normal fire truck is required, carrying a large quantity of water and foam which can be ejected within the minimum period of time. The need, therefore, is for a vehicle combining high capacity, rapid acceleration and excellent performance over difficult terrain with powerful pumps and ample turrets.

The clearance of snow from airport runways and aprons requires vehicles with ample power for both chassis and the snow-clearing gear plus sufficient traction to maintain forward movement. Normal highway snow ploughs usually work in isolation, or perhaps in tandem, but with a wide stretch of runway to keep clear it is necessary to operate the ploughs in a team of up to four or five, according to the width. The deployment of the machines across the runway depends on whether the machines have angled blades or are of the blower type. Those with a blade merely push the snow to one side, whereas the blower type churns the snow into a mass and ejects it to one side away from the runway.

Where the fall is slight the bladed plough in conjunction with gritting is sufficient, but if a blizzard develops and the depth builds up rapidly then the blower type is preferable. If the airport has several ploughs they can be arranged to work so that they each sweep adjoining strips, but with one machine only it will be necessary to make several passes to clear the required width.

Ford D1614 with high loader type body for supplying catering contracts on National Airlines Boeing 747 flights at London Heathrow.

INDUSTRIAL AND COMMERCIAL VEHICLES

In many parts of the industrial world vehicles spend their whole working lives in a contained area. These include huge logging trucks of the forests, specially shielded molten metal haulers of the foundry, large coal and ore trucks of the quarry and trucks which are assembled deep inside the mine.

Volvo F10 logging truck with stabilizers in position ready for loading with the truck-mounted hydraulic crane.

LOGGING

Trucks used in logging have by sheer necessity become some of the largest and toughest of any at work around the world, excluding those outsize machines used in mining and quarrying. Logging trucks have been developed from normal highway vehicles; but this has taken place over a considerable time, for the motor truck first started being used in the woods some time before the 1920s. Much of the early exploitation of the tall timber was carried out by men wielding axes and the fallen timber then being dragged to the river. The slow beasts of burden used for the hauling of logs to the mill or river were either oxen, elephants, mules or horses, according to the location.

In time, the stands of timber gradually receded from the river bank and the haul became too long for slow animal haulage. This meant that large areas of timber were left until mechanical transport could provide the answer. The opening up of larger areas well away from either river or sawmill was made possible by the railroads, although only a narrow gauge line could be used because of the high initial cost involved. Unfortunately, a lot of timber stands on hills, and the laying of railroad tracks is difficult in such conditions, demanding the use of frequent twists and turns to avoid the worst barriers or resorting to trestles and steep inclines to navigate the lesser obstacles. This meant the use of special locomotives and other equipment, which again was expensive.

At first the trucks were used as feeders for the more permanent railroad tracks, for they could go off at a tangent from the worked-out areas into stands of untouched timber. However, the route was bound not to be easy, for the more or less level areas would have been cut first and the trucks therefore had to handle the more difficult stands of timber.

Early logging trucks were rather primitive affairs consisting of a tough frame plus axles and engine, and little else. Work in the forest is extremely hard on any equipment, and the trucks had to deal with heavy loads, twisting tracks, roller-coaster inclines and the vagaries of mountain weather.

Failures must have been many, and much fabrication was necessary to keep the trucks operational. The sheer size of the cut timber demanded a trailer for the load, if it was not just to be dragged behind the truck. These were the days of wooden

Logging in remote areas often requires that roads be made and trestles built for the movement of logs down to the mills.

or steel wheels with solid tyres and stiff springs, and accidents on the slippery switchback forest tracks must have been frequent. On the regularly used tracks, a system of braking downhill trucks was made; cables were attached to them, wound around pulleys and then fixed to an uphill truck or to a braked winding drum.

The tracks through the woods soon became churned up; so timber roads were laid down, using either cut planks or roughly-trimmed logs. The cheapest type consisted of just two narrow 'rails' made up of sawn logs either half-buried in the soil or maybe tied together to maintain a 'track gauge'. On tricky sections it would be necessary to erect guide rails of timber to prevent the wheels sliding off the timber tracks; whereas for crossing the inevitable valleys or streams the erection of timber culverts, bridges or full-blown trestles was necessary. Naturally, for something so temporary as a logging trail, which would be of no use once the timber was cut, the construction of these bridging facilities was not carried out with any sense of permanence; and some gave way while being negotiated by the heavy logging trucks, with tragic results. Logging was a dangerous job in the early days when there was less regard for safety than there is today.

With experience the logging trucks improved and a degree of speciality developed among a handful of truck builders. In North America, Kenworth, Hayes and Pacific emerged as specialists in the logging market. In many other countries, however, the timber is of lighter proportions, and suitably modified heavy trucks are used in preference to the expensive custom-built variety.

In some areas of Washington and Oregon in North America, certain afforestations are easily reached by roads of good standard which feed directly into the public highway system. In these cases the logging trucks used conform to normal highway truck legislation so that they can move direct from the loading areas straight to the timber processing plant which may be situated up to twenty miles away.

However, where possible, it is often more economic to use the largest vehicles possible, although as they do not conform to highway regulations covering weights and dimensions they must be routed over private company roads and tracks.

Although many logging trucks do not differ

1. A Norwegian operated Volvo and trailer being loaded by the truck-mounted hydraulic grab crane.

2 Mack logging truck working in appalling conditions in Costa Rica.

3. Considerable skill and experience is required to handle heavy logging outfits in the arctic conditions of Finland.

outwardly from everyday types, they often come specified with all manner of specialist detail equipment. The braking receives special attention, for the timber often has to be collected from hillsides. In addition to standard air brakes, the logging rigs are frequently equipped with an engine brake, or retarder, and the drums are cooled by water sprinklers.

Another interesting design of the logging outfit is that the articulated type does not use a trailer as such for carrying the load. Instead the front ends of the logs are secured to a gantry positioned over the rear bogie, and the rear ends are supported by a similar gantry mounted on a 'trailer' bogie. In this way the load itself forms the 'trailer', so keeping unladen weight to a minimum. The 'trailer' bogie is maintained in its running position by a slim bar which is attached to the rear of the tractor frame, and the service lines are carried along this drawbar. When the outfit runs empty back to the pick-up point, the rear bogie can be winched up on to the tractor unit in order to save wear and make the vehicle easier to handle.

The Canadian manufacturer, Pacific Truck and Trailer Ltd, started out in 1947 to build a truck tractor aimed purely at the tough world of logging in the British Columbia area. How successful they have been in the years since that time is shown by the fact that they have extended their operations into building a line of heavy trucks for heavy hauling, oilfield work, mining and construction tasks. Orders have been met for trucks to operate in Hawaii, the USA, India, Africa, the Middle East, the Philippines, Tasmania and New Zealand. Additionally, the company was acquired by International Harvester in 1970, another recognition of their success. In the future they will continue to operate independently, although they will have access to the world-wide service and parts facilities of IHC as well as their vast research and testing facilities.

Although it is difficult to have 'standard' production trucks in such a highly-specialized field of operation as logging (for each truck is virtually hand-built), Pacific do list a handful of more or less regular standard models. They are all based on a conventional bonneted control and are of either 6×4 or 6×6 layout. Engines specified include Cummins, Detroit Diesel and Caterpillar, of outputs varying from 350 to 525 hp, but other units

can be included. A very wide range of transmissions and axles is available to meet individual requirements.

A case of an operator turning manufacturer is that of Butler Brothers Ltd, of Victoria, Southern Vancouver Island in British Columbia. A study of existing logging trucks revealed that they sometimes suffered from loss of stability by nature of their articulated layout, although this was necessary in order to obtain a long enough trailer length to take the timber lengths required. Before embarking on a large-scale building programme, Butlers discussed their proposals with the men in the woods, and finally decided on a rigid vehicle with twin steering axles for safety, plus a low height cab so that the felled timber could be carried along the vehicle without any intrusions on the load space by the cab.

The resulting vehicle is an extremely tough machine capable of carrying around 100 tons, and when it is coupled to an eight-wheeled 'pup' trailer the capacity is raised to 200 tons. This is far in excess of loads carried on the conventional articulated logging trucks, and on a return trip of around 50 or 60 miles the truck is able to make two runs per day, and therefore carries four times the amount normally returned by the regular logging outfits.

Considerable interest in the new type of logging truck has come from other lumber carriers; meanwhile Butler Brothers Equipment has plans for an even larger outfit for work in the mining industry.

1. When running empty back to the loading point, the trailer bogie is winched up partially on to the tractor unit.

2. A Hayes logging truck of MacMillan Bloedel drives out of the woods with a fair load of logs.

1

2

MINING AND QUARRYING

The extraction industries account for a substantial portion of the market for heavy vehicles; for not only are some of the heaviest production trucks used in the mining, quarrying and logging industries but some impressive heavy haulage units are often required in the initial stages when the site is being prepared and the fixed plant being installed.

Mining can be divided into two categories: deep level and surface. The equipment used in surface mining is similar to that employed in quarrying. In deep level mining, the equipment called for includes vehicles, on some occasions, but generally space is at such a premium that drilling, cutting and boring is carried on at the face, and material is carried away by conveyor or strings of rail-borne cars.

It is only in mines in which the deposits are in large areas or concentrations that vehicles are used for transportation purposes. The space available must be large enough for vehicles to manoeuvre and the ventilation system must be adequate to deal with the exhaust fumes. Therefore the operation of large vehicle fleets is confined to near-surface mines or those where the extraction takes place in a hillside and there is ready access by way of a ramp. Instances where vehicles have to be lowered down shafts or are taken down in pieces and assembled in the workings are not commonplace.

Ideally, the processing of the extracted material should take place close to the point where it is taken from the ground. This is because the load carried between these two points includes all the waste material which surrounds the commodity being extracted, and transport is expensive. To place the screening or processing plant close to the working face may be possible when the site is first opened up, but as the extraction process progresses so the working face extends farther away from the plant. Often these plants which carry out some or all of the functions of screening, sorting, cleaning, washing, grading and packaging of the desired products are considerable in their size, and once positioned they are difficult to resite. Another aspect of the positioning of the fixed plant is that it should be easily accessible from the public highway or other final transport system, for often these extraction sites are easily affected by adverse weather conditions, and roadgoing vehicles may find access across unmade tracks impossible. For safety

1

2

1. The German Faun range of dump trucks is available in models from 18 to 85 tonnes' payload.

2. Opencast or strip mining can be carried out quite close to the surface. On other occasions the coal seam may be at a considerable depth, which means that trucks have a long climb up from the loading site.

3. Volvo N12 6×4 dumper heading out of a mine with its load.

reasons, it is best to keep the working site area free from all superfluous traffic and pedestrians, especially if the extraction involves the use of explosives.

The type of equipment used to extract the material will be determined by several criteria, including its general accessibility, the amount to be extracted, the value of the commodity, the thickness of the seam, the type of material being sought and the surrounding soil. Obviously, extracting vast quantities of hard granite will require tougher equipment than digging out Fullers Earth. Similarly, a huge gravel working will require a lot more equipment than a tiny sandstone quarry. The mining of deep-seated iron ore requires one set of equipment, whereas salt mining requires another.

Where the desired material abounds in huge quantities and the demand for it is high, there will be economic sense in installing massive extraction machines such as the walking draglines employed in some of the open-cast coal mines, clay workings for brick-making etc. The capacity of these huge machines may be at such a high level that no ordi-

Foden dump truck working in the ICI salt mine at Winsford. The vehicle had to be assembled inside the mine.

nary dump trucks could cope with their output, and it may be necessary to install a continuous-service rail/car link with the processing plant or to install a conveyor to remove the material.

In smaller quarries the demand for the material may be subject to variations or the site so physically limited that a small bucket excavator kept serviced by a fleet of average-size dump trucks can adequately fill the bill.

Between these extremes comes a whole host of specialist and varying applications for excavators, loaders, dump trucks and ancillary equipment which is exemplified by the wide range of vehicles and equipment offered by an array of manufacturers.

MOLTEN METAL CARRIAGE

1

3

Another unusual type of vehicle is that used within the confines of a steel-works for handling liquid metal in giant ladles. The vehicle is equipped with a pair of pivoting arms which hinge away from the rear of the vehicle load platform to engage with two lifting pins on the ladle. By hydraulic power the loaded ladle is lifted on to the vehicle and then transported to the moulding shop. Here the vehicle is manoeuvred up to the moulds and the ladle contents emptied out by tipping. The vehicle then returns to the smelting shop for another full ladle.

The vehicle cab has two sets of controls. For moving the vehicle from one point to another, the driver uses what one would term the normal set of controls, situated at the front of the cab. The positioning of the vehicle for picking up and tipping the contents requires great precision, and for this purpose a second set of rearward-facing controls is provided.

Construction of the vehicle is generally not dissimilar to that of a roadgoing truck, except that the rear axles have solid tyres and limited-movement

1. This special Foden tractor unit which operates within the confines of Llanwern British Steel works carrying scrap is rated at 135 tons gross.

2. Foden FC20 dump truck chassis converted to a tractor unit for operation with steel coil carrying trailer.

3. Designed for highway use as well as within the works, this special Foden outfit carries scrap and slag for British Steel.

suspension. Because of the great heat encountered by the vehicle as it traverses the smelting area, a skirt is provided to protect the tyres from burning. At the load-carrying end of the vehicle this skirt extends right down to ground level by means of a flexible curtain. The back and roof of the cab are protected from excessive heat and spillage of the ladle contents by insulation and metal shields.

1

2

3

1. *Specially built Foden Tractor unit with solid tyred semi trailer for the internal works transport of coiled steel at the British Steel Shotton Works.*

2. *DJB D330 and D275 model dump trucks outside the works awaiting delivery. Currently some 90 per cent of production goes for export.*

3. *This rear end view gives some idea of the size of the largest dump truck – the Terex Titan.*

4. *The tight operating conditions imposed upon trucks working in deep mines is clearly shown by this view of a Volvo N10 dump truck working far underground.*

ROAD/RAIL TRUCKS

Although regarded mainly as competitors, the railroads are in many ways large users of road vehicles. In some parts of the world large fleets of trucks are operated as local distribution and feeder services. Some railway companies actually own and operate such fleets purely as road transport operators, competing directly with the legal road haulage network. Less familiar are the special vehicles which the railways use as service and breakdown vehicles, including such specialized items as rail grinders, locomotive and rolling stock servicers, wrecking cranes, wagon shunters and wheel changers.

It seems ironical that railways have to rely upon road vehicles for so much of their operation, but often it makes good sense to use a motor vehicle which is so flexible in operation that it can vary its route at short notice if required. When accidents occur, a truck is able to move all around the scene whereas the rail-borne wrecking crane is restricted to its rails. Another advantage of the road truck is its ability to work close to the track without impeding the flow of rail traffic. In addition, if there are several tasks to be done on different lines, it is able to proceed across country to another branch without having to return to a junction each time.

For the best of both worlds, as it were, some vehicles have been built on the road/rail principle so that they may travel by the most expedient route and then work either from the railroad track or alongside it, as the case may decide. Trucks with the ability to travel over the road or along the tracks are not new. There have been many trials in the past aimed at producing a dual-purpose vehicle which could be quickly transferred from road to rail or vice versa and which did not cost the earth. Some of the designs have been extremely complicated, heavy and expensive, and have found little commercial use. In recent years there have been fresh thoughts concerning this type of vehicle, and the trend has been toward a model which is primarily a road vehicle but which has additional small wheels used merely to locate the vehicle on the rail track. Propulsion is still provided by the roadgoing wheels which rely upon the weight of the vehicle to give the necessary adhesion on the rail tops. With this system there is no need to resort to complicated and expensive dual-drive wheel arrangements, and there is an added bonus in that the changeover time is drastically reduced. The use of hydraulic rams

1

2

1, 2, 3, 4. The comparative simplicity of the German Zweiweg system for converting normal road-going vehicles into rail-borne trucks is shown in this selection of railway maintenance and shunting units. Although Mercedes Benz vehicles are shown, almost any truck which falls within the design parameters could be converted in this manner.

3

4

has meant that the movement of the flanged rail wheels is much more swift than was the case with the older type of vehicles, which relied upon cumbersome eccentric mountings.

With the new, simplified system of providing railgoing ability for trucks it is possible to adapt normal production vehicles at a reasonable cost; so now railroad maintenance gangs have a light truck which is able to use whichever surface is most expedient. Loading might take place in the maintenance yard and the truck set off over the road to a remote stretch of track not directly connected to the main system. When the job is complete, the truck could perhaps take to the rails for a task which is located in a cutting or somewhere where there is no road access. Upon completion of the day's work, the vehicle would return to base by the most direct route.

Other vehicles in this category could be an emergency truck or one equipped with fire apparatus. These would have much greater flexibility of operation through being able to negotiate both roads and rail tracks. One such vehicle is operated by a railway system in which a considerable amount of track runs through tunnels. Should an emergency arise the vehicle is initially despatched by road, switching to rail at the nearest surface access point to the trouble spot.

1

1. In this view of a Zweiweg conversion the tiny rail bogies can be clearly seen.

2. Foremost Commander desert crossing vehicle carrying a D7 Caterpillar dozer to a site across difficult conditions for normal vehicles.

2

RUBBISH DISPOSAL

Rubbish, refuse, garbage, call it what you will, this vast by-product of modern society increases in amount as each year passes. It was not so long ago that organized rubbish disposal did not exist. In the age of wood and coal burning fires, furnaces and boilers, it was a relatively simple problem to dispose of unwanted packaging etc – simple, that was, until we became more aware of our smog-laden atmosphere and the health hazards created by pollution of the air. It was also quite easy for industries to rid themselves of their unwanted by-products and waste. If it was solid and non-combustible it was merely piled up in open country in the hope that the grass might one day cover its ugly contour, or perhaps that it might even be useful in the future. With liquid waste it was even easier – dump it in the river or the sea.

As far as the town dweller was concerned, the organized disposal of rubbish began around the middle of the nineteenth century, but many country areas had to wait much longer before they saw regular refuse collection. In some areas even now people are expected to make their own arrangements for normal rubbish. In quite recent times there have even been differing views on rubbish disposal, with some authorities wanting to collect it all and then try to recuperate some of the collection cost by salvaging some materials, whereas others urged householders to burn all they could, so reducing the bulk and therefore the cost of collection. This state of affairs could not continue after the various anti-pollution laws were enacted, for these entirely prohibited the burning of anything slightly smoke-producing. These same laws have been instrumental in causing local authorities to dispense with their own giant incineration plants, with the result that landfill programmes have come into prominence for rubbish disposal.

Other problems have reared their heads in recent times, for as our towns have expanded the inner reclamation sites have become filled and the search for new sites has spread ever wider. Whereas at one time the actual refuse collection vehicle could leave its round in order to dump its load at the tip, in many areas this is just no longer possible. The dumping site is so far from the towns that special bulk vehicles have to be engaged purely for the 'trunking' operation, which again adds to the collection cost because of the double handling involved. Huge transfer stations are set up (perhaps on a collective basis serving several local authorities) in order to handle the transhipment of the refuse, and in some instances these are on the sites of the defunct incinerators.

In some cases it has been possible to move the refuse by barges if the reclamation area is adjacent to the river, and there is at least one scheme where complete trains of special rubbish containers perform a shuttle service from transfer station to landfill site, a distance of about thirty miles!

All this upheaval in the rubbish disposal business has brought about demands for some pretty large vehicles for the transfer of the load from town to tip. Refuse is basically a bulky load with little weight in relation to cubic capacity in its raw state. In order to move it as cheaply as possible, the compressor type of body has been in use for many years. Original moving-barrier types have gradually given way to more sophisticated designs which utilize paddles, screws, hydraulic rams and other ingenious devices aimed at getting the proverbial quart into a pint pot! The vehicles used for the actual transfer operation, however, do not normally carry such equipment; they rely on receiving the rubbish in a compressed state from special high-density packers installed at the transfer point. Even so, some of the transfer vehicles have to be of maximum proportions in order to move the greatest loads.

In some instances vehicle operators have turned their attention to using the demountable type of body for refuse work, for this allows maximum utilization of the motive unit during loading operations. In addition, some tip sites can be extremely

1 and 2. The generous proportions of the special Kaelble refuse transfer trucks can be gauged from these photographs. With a capacity of 100 cubic metres the trucks are almost twice as wide as the conventional refuse collection vehicles which tip their contents into these huge demountable bodies at the transfer station. Side discharge makes for a lower overall height when tipping on site.

1

2

1

2

3

1. Foremost 'Magnum Four' low profile cross-country truck loaded with six sections of 80 foot length 42-inch diameter pipe.

2. Foremost 'Husky 8' tracked cargo truck used on oilfield duties in Indonesia.

3. Faun of Germany offer a wide range of off-highway equipment for oilfield work. This model HZ.36.40/45 prime mover is available in 6×6 form with a choice of engines up to 1000 hp.

4. Australian Kenworth SAR type being loaded with roadstone by a Caterpillar wheeled loader.

5. A pilot model of Euclid Ch–150 bottom discharge dump truck at work in the Peabody Coal Universal Mine near Terre Haute.

4

5

hazardous for normal roadgoing trucks, because the site is often covered with refuse which has merely been discharged by tipping, without any subsequent compression taking place.

Another problem arises with the use of articulated vehicles, which are often specified in order to obtain large loads. Tipping such high vehicles can be very tricky, particularly on uneven surfaces such as exist on tip sites, and there is the additional risk of the load sticking in the body during tipping, which can lead to disaster as the vehicle becomes unstable.

By using demountable bodies or skips, the transfer vehicle can deposit its body complete with load in an area adjacent to the tip, leaving the actual tipping operation to a special site truck with regular trained staff. The rubbish is then bulldozed where required, or covered with a layer of special 'soil' laced with chemicals aimed at achieving rapid decomposition.

Although the transfer vehicles are of maximum size for roadgoing operation, at least one manufacturer has come up with even bigger vehicles for the handling of the loads within the landfill site. Although this means another handling operation, it does provide a site vehicle which is specially designed for stability and maximum capacity without the encumbrances of the wings, lights, dimensions and weights demanded for road operation.

The West German specialist truck builder, Carl Kaelble, has recently introduced this design of high-capacity site-dumper with demountable body. Employing a rigid six-wheel chassis carried on low-pressure tyres, the extra wide vehicle carries its 100 cubic metre open body on a special side-tipping subframe. It is basically about twice the width of a normal truck, and the body is specially shaped to assist the discharge of the load during tipping.

The fitting of a centre stabilizer is prudent for heavy tipping vehicles working on the dubious surfaces found in refuse tips.

COAL HAULING

In the specialized field of coal hauling, normal off-highway type dump trucks are not widely used, as the very nature of the load requires that vehicles are built to a more specific requirement.

In countries like Britain the majority of coal is mined from underground workings, and once the coal has been hauled to the surface and processed it is usually transported away by the railways which operate wagon sidings right to the pithead. However, in some countries of the world (America, for instance), much of the coal is obtained from open-cast workings, where once the earth and foliage covering has been removed the coal can be readily scraped away in layers. Such workings usually call for off-highway trucks with bigger than average load capacities, as the lightweight nature of coal compared with, say, granite or limestone means that the maximum operational weight of a 100-ton dump truck could never be approached before the body had been filled.

Over the years two main types of coal-hauling dump trucks have been developed, one a rigid straight truck design and the other a tractor/semi-trailer combination. The rigid truck is usually a big, long wheelbase 6×4 vehicle with a long dump body equipped with high sides so that a high volume of coal can be loaded, often as much as 50 tons at a time.

American vehicles tend to dominate the large-size coal-hauling truck market, and Mack trucks were one of the market leaders in this field until this manufacturer from Allentown, Pennsylvania, pulled out of the off-highway arena early in 1979. With the demise of the Mack M-series, the market is now dominated by such 50-tonners as Kenworth 548 and Cline 250C. Although relatively unheard of outside America, Cline has actually been in the truck manufacturing business for some twenty-six years. Recently, it has been the target for various

Special Australian type of Mack eight-wheel tractor unit coupled to a high capacity tipping trailer.

1. *The usefulness of the truck-mounted hydraulic crane for tasks such as pylon rigging and power line maintenance is well proven by their service with the power supply companies.*

2. *Truck-mounted rig carrying out conventional dynamite type seismic survey in Cheshire for Shell UK Exploration in 1978. Alongside the drilling rig is a water tanker.*

take-overs (and was for a short while known as
ISCO).

Whereas the 22 foot long and 12 foot wide body
of the Cline 250C can handle, say, a heaped 60
cubic yards of coal, its bigger brother the Cline
C265 can handle a bulky 73 cubic yards. The C265
is a 65-ton capacity coal hauler which is powered by
a Cummins KTA 1150-C600 diesel rated at
600 bhp at 2100 rpm, and this beast of the coalfields
runs on massive 1800×25 tyres.

For hauling king-size loads of coal, even bigger
trucks are needed, and companies such as Euclid,
Mack and Terex have developed huge articulated
tractor/semi-trailer rigs based on their various
off-highway dump truck chassis. The 120-ton
capacity Euclid CH120 series rig is based on the
Euclid R85 85-ton capacity rigid dump truck chassis, although the CH tractor version offers only the
installation of a V12 Cummins 1710 diesel rated at
either 700 or 800 bhp.

The heaviest off-highway Mack 4×2 dump
truck, the 65-ton capacity M65AX, provided the
basis for that company's 120-ton capacity coal-
hauling rig. Mack also offered their own 'Mack
Trailer Train' specialist rigs which centred around
the M75SX 6×4 dump truck chassis operating as a
semi-tractor. Whereas this tractor can only handle
one trailer with its 700 bhp Detroit diesel or 800
bhp Cummins engine, the 'Trailer Train' set-up
allows for the addition of several power dollies to be
coupled on to the rear of each trailer allowing for
multiple trailer configurations. Payloads of up to
400 tons are therefore possible with the use of such
'trains'.

The largest Mack dump truck to leave the draw-
ing boards of Allentown and reach the erecting
halls was the M100SX 100-ton capacity 6×4,
although this vehicle could never be said to be
designated as a coal hauler. The Terex 34-11C coal
hauler is powered by an 880 bhp Detroit Diesel and
rated at 150 short tons (136,100 kg), and with the
general rate of progress at Terex it may not be long
before an articulated version of the Terex Titan
emerges with maybe a 500-ton load capacity!

Euclid B–110 articulated dumper.

DRILLING RIGS

In man's frenzied search for supplies of fuel the quest for oil has attracted more special equipment and vehicles than any other. Trucks for seismological testing, geological exploration, well drilling, rig servicing and all the ancillary transport require huge capital investment. They are special in the extreme.

*The difficulties encountered by drilling rig crews is
illustrated by this view of a hillside bore being made
by a Lockheed mounted rig.*

The mobile drilling rig is another highly specialized piece of equipment which has come into great prominence in recent years because of the emphasis being placed on the urgent quest for energy supplies. With so many countries now striving for a place in the modern industrial world, the demand for fuel from the long-established sources has reached huge proportions. No longer can we assume that the existing coal, oil and gas supplies are inexhaustible; and all over the globe exploration is proceeding at an unprecedented rate in a bid to locate and extract previously untapped supplies.

It is not only in the search for fuel that the drilling rig finds use, for with world population constantly expanding there is a very real need for additional areas to be given over to food production. With this increased pressure upon the accepted arable areas, agriculturalists are now turning their attention to hitherto untilled ground which might yield healthy crops, provided that there is sufficient and regular rainfall. This is precisely where the drilling rigs come in useful, for so often the ground is barren through lack of rain and water has to be obtained from below ground, often at depths of several hundred feet.

Whether it be for oil, gas or water exploration, the drilling rig vehicle is the same in outline. What is required is a substantial chassis capable of taking the drilling tower and equipment to the site, which is invariably located well away from highways, and indeed sometimes is deep inside a forest, desert or rocky region. Therefore the chassis frame must be of generous proportions if the equipment carried is not to suffer through transport over difficult terrain. Obviously, for a completely inaccessible area, the equipment would have to be lifted in by air, or at very least the vehicle would have to be fully or partially tracked. Alternatively, in the case of swampy ground, the rig would have to be mounted on low pressure flotation type tyres.

The large majority of rigs, however, are carried on trucks with a three- or four-axle configuration with at least two axles being powered. Obviously a vehicle with all axles driven is sometimes desirable,

Although not what is normally associated with drilling operations this Polecat hole borer is none the less a useful tool for the rapid drilling of many shallow bores.

1

but as this feature adds considerably to the weight and cost of the unit it will not be specified unless really necessary. Another problem of drive axles is that of a limited ground clearance, and this has to be taken into account, although usually the site will have been visited earlier and an assessment made as to the suitability of the equipment in use. Often the first serious study of the area in general, and the drilling site in particular, will have been made by a seismographic survey unit itself carried on a special off-highway vehicle.

In order to obtain a large frame top area for the equipment, the chassis will have a forward-set cab together with the motive power unit. The drilling tower itself is set at the extreme rear of the chassis frame, and it is raised from the horizontal travelling position and positioned vertically for the drilling operation by means of a pair of hydraulic rams. It is essential that the drilling tower maintains a vertical aspect, and that any flexibility produced by the vehicle tyres or suspension does not interfere with a truly vertical bore being maintained. Two hydraulic legs or stabilizers are mounted close to the base of the tower at the rear of the vehicle to

ensure that the tower maintains a vertical attitude laterally, while a single stabilizer or a pair of stabilizers is mounted at the front of the chassis to provide longitudinal alignment.

Power for the drilling operation is provided by a large diesel engine which is usually mounted on top of the vehicle chassis, and positioned either centrally or to the front in order to maintain the desired axle loadings in motive use. This engine must have a large radiator if water cooling is employed, for it may be required to operate for considerable periods at quite high ambient temperatures, such as those encountered when drilling in tropical areas.

Other equipment carried on the vehicle centres mainly around the drilling function, with tank for engine fuel, lubricants and water supplies plus hydraulic fluid tank, and lockers for the storage of numerous loose tools and spare parts as required. Larger items of equipment are usually brought to the site by separate supply vehicles or helicopters as necessary.

Most oil-drilling is done in desert regions, which demand special trucks, as now described.

1. *In direct contrast to the photograph on page 133 is this highly specialized Foremost fully tracked oilfield truck of the late 1970s.*

2. *Mobile drilling rig mounted on a Bedford 4 ×4 chassis.*

OILFIELD TRUCKING

There is perhaps just a handful of truck manu-facturers building trucks to the heavyweight oilfield specification, including such names as Oshkosh, Berliet, PRP, Kenworth, MOL, Magirus Deutz and Scammell. Kenworth are without doubt the market leaders in this field of operation. Their huge 953 series truck and tractor range is built at the Kansas City Paccar Plant, the nearest to the Texan oilfields.

The American Oshkosh truck manufacturer builds both 4×4 and 6×6 trucks, designed to operate in the desert; and the 325 bhp Caterpillar diesel-powered 6×6 Oshkosh Desert Prince truck has a brochure which proudly claims that 'the

Desert Prince takes on the harsh environment of sand and sun ... and calls it home!' For such a relatively small company, the Wisconsin-based manufacturer has taken over portions of various truck markets around the world, spreading the name of the Oshkosh Red Indian tribe far and wide.

PRP is the latest name for another stalwart of the desert trucking scene, the Willème. When the French Willème company went to the wall some years ago the manufacturing rights were taken over by the local General Motors agent who had already been supplying diesels to the manufacturer. The company has flourished, and recently the directors

Some truck builders such as Scammells have been producing special trucks for oilfield use since the 1920s.

of Perez and Raimond Paris SA decided to use their own company's initials on the trucks in favour of the outmoded Willème badge. The W8 SAAR 6×6 PRP tractor has a gross weight of 75,000 kg and is powered by the 318 bhp version of the Detroit Diesel 8V71 series engine driving through the evergreen Fuller RTO 9513 13-speed gearbox.

The Belgian truck manufacturer MOL builds a variety of 4×4 and 6×6 off-highway vehicles including the T6066 extra heavy duty truck. MOL readily admits that the basic concept for their oilfield trucks stems from the much admired and popular Kenworth 953, although they aim to take the design a stage further and incorporate, in their

1

opinion, some better options in this field.

Power for the Mighty MOL 6×6 comes from the V12 Deutz BF12L 413 type air-cooled diesel which seems ideally suited to the waterless arid wastes of any desert. MOL engineers have incorporated in the engine some novel devices of their own manufacturer, such as air jets driven from the truck's air tanks. These regularly blast away at the Deutz-finned cylinder blocks in order to keep them free from grit and sand, which could clog up the fins and impede the engine's cooling ability.

Although the West German Company Magirus Deutz are not as yet up into the real super heavyweight league when it comes to constructing desert specification trucks, they are certainly pushing their rivals hard, and the Deutz air-cooled diesel engines are definitely at home in the hot and dry conditions. Magirus Deutz 6×6 dump trucks are noted performers through deep mud, and the big 'Maggies' found in the Sahara Desert are certainly proving their worth.

In the 1950s and 1960s the British-built Scammell 'Constructor' and 'Super Constructor' 6×6 trucks and tractors virtually ruled the desert

1. Scammell 'Constructor' 6×6 with a trailer load of drilling equipment rolls off a barge on its way to a job for the Iraq Petroleum Co.

2. Even in the wide open spaces of the desert accidents happen, as this 4×4 Oshkosh recovery vehicle shows.

3. Berliet GXO model 6×6 with V16 540 hp engine at work on an oilfield project hauling pumping equipment. The vehicle operates at a gross weight of 150 tonnes.

2

3

1

domain and could be found working for almost every Middle Eastern oilfield. The very nature of oilfield trucking calls for very robust trucks which, having been loaded with maybe 30, 40 or even 50 tons of drilling rig directly on to the back, can still churn their way across soft sand. Although Scammell are still involved in the production of desert specification trucks, today they seem to be aiming more directly at the heavy hauling and tank transporter markets, as opposed to the specialized oilfield vehicles.

On the other side of the world, the hot sandy desert areas of Texas have been providing equally difficult trucking conditions. These have been successfully met by Foremost Industries, a company which specializes in the construction of huge off-highway trucks which are equally at home in the desert as they are on the snowy wastes of America's latest huge oilfield in Alaska. Designing and constructing heavyweight trucks for oilfield transportation needs has enabled Foremost to steer away from normal highway truck derivatives, thus producing very specialized vehicles indeed. Wheeled and tracked trucks are built at plants in Houston,

Texas, and Alberta, Canada, with both production facilities being right on top of their respective market outlets.

Two-, three- and four-axle wheeled straight trucks are offered, all of which feature all-wheel drive and huge soft balloon terra tyres which enable the trucks to cross the most difficult of terrain. Trucks such as the Foremost 'Commander' 6×6 have centre frame steering, and offer payloads of up to 27 tonnes on a platform deck some 2 metres from the ground. A Detroit Diesel 8V71T series turbocharged engine rated at 350 bhp powers the 'Commander' at speeds of up to 20 mph.

Whereas the Foremost 'Commander' and its slightly smaller brothers the 6×6 'Delta 3' and 4×4 'Delta 2' are aimed at the general freight and support vehicle field of oilfield transportation, the monstrous four-axle, 8×8 drive 'Magnum 4' truck is built specifically for hauling the huge pipes used in the construction of pipelines across the most unforgiving terrain. The 'Magnum 4' is the largest wheeled truck in the Foremost range and is powered by a Detroit Diesel 12V71T turbocharged diesel developing some 465 bhp. The 8×8 truck is supported on eight huge Goodyear Super Terra 66×43×25 tyres mounted on earthmover rims, and has a platform-loading height of 98 inches from the ground.

1. The Canadian Foremost company builds a variety of highly specialized equipment for the construction and oilfield industries. This is their Delta Three, a three axle articulated load carrier with low pressure tyres for sand or swamp use.

2. The Lockheed company also produce special vehicles to cope with the difficulties experienced with transportation of equipment in remote areas such as Alaska and the north of Canada.

With a cab and engine mounted beneath the loading deck, huge oilfield pipes can overhang both the front and the rear of the truck. Constructed to haul up to six 80 foot long, 48 inch diameter pipes at a time, the 'Magnum 4' truck can handle up to 63,500 kg of load under off-highway conditions.

Obviously there are sticky conditions, such as swamps, rivers and even bogs, where even the most tractable wheeled truck will eventually get bogged down, and to combat these conditions Foremost Industries construct a variety of tracked vehicles. With load capacities of 3,600 right up to 36,000 kg, these rather unusual articulating trucks are capable of carrying loads where other trucks would not dare to venture. Rivers, swamps and bogs present little problem to these highly flexible machines, which can wade through 6 feet of water without the platform deck becoming awash.

The 'Husky 8' is the largest tracked truck currently in production by Foremost, and it is powered by a Cummins 855 diesel rated at 335 bhp, which drives through a 4-speed Allison Automatic gearbox, giving the truck a top speed of 10 mph.

2

CRANES

The spectacular growth of the construction industry in terms of pure size has demanded greater capacity equipment in every direction, and is particularly notable in the case of the truck-mounted crane. It has grown from a humble machine of around 5 tons' capacity to being able to lift 1000 tons!

The 500-ton capacity Gottwald crane of Sparrows being used to erect a dockside crane in 1973.

Cranes used on construction sites vary considerably in size and use, from the small capacity truck-mounted grab for loading of loose material, through the static tower cranes for handling almost every job on a building project, to the mobile hydraulic job cranes which are used for specific purposes and have capacities right up to 1000 tons.

The largest cranes generally in use are those in shipbuilding. In the land transport field the biggest were those used by the railways for righting derailed locomotives. In construction work the cranes are usually of the static fixed type, although in recent years there has been tremendous growth in the mobile or truck-mounted crane field. For infrequent lifting tasks the truck-mounted crane is ideal, for it can be rapidly despatched to the required site, and after the job is complete equally swiftly moved to another job or returned to the depot. Because of the intermittent use of these high-cost items of equipment, there has been a trend towards specialist crane hire firms who carry a stock of cranes of varying size, reach and capacity to handle a wide variety of lifting tasks at almost a

moment's notice of the job required.

As with transport, the crane business can vary enormously, and often the two work closely on many projects. The cranes called for on various jobs are of many different types. One job may be to lift a heavy piece of machinery into position through a narrow doorway, or under an arch, but on a solid foundation. Another task might well be to handle the siting of a new railway bridge over a road at the dead of night. Yet another job might entail positioning a comparatively lightweight item like a water tank or chimney section on top of a tower block. Often the actual lifting and positioning takes little time; it is the preparation and setting up of the equipment which takes time. In addition to this, the setting up of the crane, which might entail positioning on the public highway and then adding extra boom sections, often results in the closure of the highway. Local authorities might well demand that this operation be carried out over a holiday period or weekend, in the case of a city development, or even during the night if the road is normally heavily used during daylight hours.

Although hardly qualifying for the term 'crane',

1

in recent years there has been a great increase in the fitting of small-capacity lifting jibs direct on to ordinary trucks. These are really an extension of the trend of mechanical handling throughout industry and they have proved to be extremely efficient and economic. Whereas previously one had to rely on a separate mobile crane to load the vehicle at a site or a fixed overhead crane at a factory, or even a gang of strong-armed men with shovels, today the driver-operated vehicle crane is capable of doing the job independently. Obviously, the load has to be accessible to the vehicle, or at least within reach of its crane. This factor, however, is not too restrictive when one studies the specification of modern truck-mounted cranes, for some types are offered with a reach up to 40 feet, bearing in mind of course that the lifting capacity of cranes diminishes with increases in horizontal reach.

Another important point with regard to the operation of vehicle-mounted equipment is the need to protect the vehicle itself adequately from the forces created as lifting takes place. This protection usually takes the form of outriggers, legs,

1. *Foden CC8–12/30 crane carrier chassis with Bucyrus Erie 45C crane mounted. This model featured the special design of cab made solely for Bucyrus Erie.*

2. *Grove 70-ton capacity telescopic crane with lattice extension at work on a microwave radio tower.*

jacks or stabilizers, which make a rigid connection between the crane base or the vehicle chassis and the ground. This relieves the chassis and its suspension and tyres of any sudden increases in point loads, occasioned by the crane, for example, picking up a tonne load at a radius of some 6 metres. Even if an unstabilized vehicle did not turn over, it could at least suffer broken suspension or a twisted chassis frame.

The most common form of lorry-mounted crane is that of between 1- and 2-tonne capacity for operation at around 4 to 6 metres' radius, mounted immediately behind the cab. These are used widely in the construction and supplies industries for delivering all types of materials to sites. They also come into use for loading loose materials on to the vehicle, in such instances as site clearance or the removal of debris from a hole dug in the road; and in those instances a grab or clamshell is used in place of a plain hook.

Other specialized uses of the truck loader are achieved by fitting either a pair of forks, so that it can pick up a pallet load of material, or a pair of clamps, which can handle a stack of bricks or building blocks. By installing a multi-tine or timber type grab, the loader can handle loose timber or lengths of piping. By installing slings or spreaders, all manner of loads can be handled, and there have been instances of a cage being installed so that an operative can clean high fixtures or change light fittings.

As mentioned earlier, these truck loaders are usually mounted behind the vehicle cab. Owing to the problem of lessening capacity at some of the longer reaches, however, it has become necessary to mount the loader in the middle of the vehicle body in instances where there is a long load platform. In this way the loader works from the centre, picking the items from front and rear and from one side or the other in order to maintain stability and lessen the risk of frame twisting. Naturally, outriggers or jacks have to be positioned so as to relieve the chassis of the vehicle from any loading stress.

Another variation on the truck-loader theme has been the moving gantry type of loader. This takes the form of a rigid overhead gantry which spans the vehicle load area and can run the length of the body by means of rails running down the extreme edges.

The truck-mounted crane has been in existence for about sixty years, for it was during World War 1

Atkinson 6×4 crane carrier chassis with Rapier lattice boom crane stowed alongside halfcab for road running. Boom extensions are carried on the nearside.

that Thew-Lorain in America took to mounting a self-contained grab-bucket loader on to an AC model Mack. During the 1920s there was an increased demand for vehicles of this type for use in the rapidly expanding construction industry. With the lack of the high pressure hydraulic ram, however, the operation of the cranes and grabs of the period revolved around the established methods in which a petrol engine supplied power direct to a winding drum and the operation was conducted via wire ropes.

The next step came with the use of an electric generator driven by a separate engine or that of the vehicle, which supplied power for an electrically-driven crane. Because of the high weights of these early items of equipment, the chassis were usually carried on solid rubber tyres.

Many of the very early mobile cranes had no cab at all so that the crane could be slewed in any direction, as well as leaving ample room for the boom to be stowed up front while the vehicle was on the move. By the 1930s, a cab was being fitted to the vehicles and the boom rested on top, or a half cab was provided with the boom nestling alongside.

The production of mobile cranes was continued during World War 2 in order to speed up the fabrication of military installations, and the military themselves made good use of such items of equipment in the field of operations when establishing supply depots, fuelling facilities or aircraft servicing points.

Very many of the ex-military machines continued in service after the war and continue to do so even today, a fact which reflects highly on their designers and builders. Obviously, the wartime cranes were of limited capacity. With the vast increase in industrialization in the period following the war, the demand for greater numbers of cranes, coupled with the tremendous increase in the size of loads to be lifted, paved the way for the giant machines available today. Moreover, the end has still not been reached; for a mobile truck-mounted crane with a capacity of 1000 tonnes was due for delivery to Sparrows International during 1979. This monster crane, built by Leo Gottwald, is designed to handle extremely heavy lifts which have become almost commonplace with the expansion of the construction and petro-chemical industries. Although heavy lifts have been carried out in

the past, these have necessitated the use of two or more cranes. Sparrows are confident that, although more than £2 million has been invested in this new world-beater, considerable savings will be achieved by using just one unit in the future.

Nevertheless, although such giants of the mobile lifting world are interesting, they are by no means commonplace, and most of the units produced come within much smaller capacities.

Atkinson Vehicles made a brief entry into the crane carrier market during the 1960s, when they offered a variety of options based on a six-wheel (6×4) chassis. There was a choice of wheelbase, engine, gearbox and other items, including a single offset cab or twin cabs where the crane jib nestled between the two. The crane base was mounted over the Kirkstall bogie and the chassis was catalogued as being suitable for a variety of cranes by Jones, Ruston Bucyrus and Rapier.

The capacity of the chassis was up to 27 tons gross, with an overall length of 21 ft 5 in, and it had I-section side rails of 12 in×8 in, 14 in×8 in or 20 in×6.5 in, as opposed to the channel section used on the normal highway type vehicles. Naturally, the actual lifting capacity of the crane mounted varied considerably, and whereas on some vehicles the crane boom was maintained complete for highway journeys on others only the bottom section of the boom remained in situ and the additional sections were carried between the cab and the crane base. In other cases the booms were capable of being hinged in two for road journeys to avoid excessive frontal overhang.

Founded only as recently as 1953, the Crane Carrier Company has established itself as a leading builder of specialist truck chassis for the mounting of transit mixers, cranes, drilling rigs, dumpers and oil-well servicing rigs. In addition, the company also produces a line of chassis for the more orthodox work of highway tractors, refuse trucks and other bulk haulers. Another part of the truck market has recently been explored by the production of a vehicle named the Custom Block Hauler, which embodies a six-wheel chassis with a half-cab and a flat body with a hydraulic crane mounted at the extreme rear of the frame. As its name implies, the vehicle is designed specially for the handling of bricks or building blocks in palletized lots. A similar chassis is used for mounting dump bodies and concrete mixers.

One of Sparrows' Gottwald cranes being used to position prestressed concrete beams on a new highway bridge.

Although the company does list certain standard models in its catalogue, CCC is primarily a builder of custom trucks, so there is a considerable choice with regard to equipment. The roadgoing models generally have channel frames of bolted construction, whereas those designed for off-highway or site use come with I-beam side rails and the chassis frame is of all-welded construction.

The concrete mixer chassis are designed for gross weights of between 54,000 and 140,000 lb and body capacities of 6.5 to 20 cubic yards, and are available in 6×4, 6×6 and 8×4 configurations.

Crane-carrier chassis have either I-beam or box section frames, and can accommodate 15- to 200-ton capacity cranes. In addition to the highway type of crane carrier, a railroad wrecking crane is also produced, with special four-man crew cab. This vehicle is constructed for travel on the highway as well as on railroad tracks.

Douglas Equipment of Cheltenham have been concerned with the production of a wide variety of special vehicles during their history. At one time they were producing chassis which embodied the all-wheel-drive line of driven and steering axles, and these were used for crane carriers, aircraft crash tenders, logging trucks, dumping trucks and snow ploughs as well as all-wheel-drive conversions of conventional rear-wheel-drive vehicles.

Aircraft cargo handling vehicles, aircraft tugs, oil drilling equipment, oil prospecting equipment, terminal tractors, exploration vehicles and even bus chassis have all been produced by this specialist building firm, which was established in 1947.

The crane-carrier chassis was available in 4×2, 4×4, 6×4 or 6×6 forms, and came complete with an all-welded I-beam section frame with screw-jack type outriggers. The standard engine was the Perkins R6V, rated at 108 bhp, and a half-cab was fitted. Capacities were listed as 5 to 35 tons' lift.

Faun-Werke of Germany produce a whole range of crane-carrier chassis. This range forms just one section of a wider sphere of special vehicles used in the construction, engineering, oilfield, fire-fighting and municipal fields.

The construction of crane-carrier chassis began before 1939, but these were really normal road-going chassis with an additional sub-frame to carry the crane ring gear and superstructure. During the post-war period, production of these chassis began

again, although by today's standards they were puny machines of capacities of around 10 tonnes. This contrasts sharply with the powerful lifts obtainable today.

The modern range encompasses many different types, from a 6×4 with a tonne/metre capacity of just 60 right up to a 16×8 layout with a maximum lift of 500 tonnes, or 2,500 tonne/metres.

Faun place great faith in the Deutz air-cooled diesel engines, and these are a standard fitment right throughout the crane carrier range, except for the two largest models which have either Cummins or Daimler-Benz units.

The production of special Foden chassis for transit cranes extended from 1948 to 1975, during which period some 700 units were built. Most of the vehicles were produced at the Sandbach works, but a limited number were assembled at other plants both in the UK and in other nations.

Early production of crane carriers centred around the use of normal roadgoing chassis suitably strengthened around the parts of greatest stress, such as the rear bogie/turntable ring area. In the period following World War 2 mobile cranes were of limited capacity, but with the expansion of building contracts during the 1950s there was increasing demand for greater lifting capacities. To this end the crane chassis were given chassis frame members of rolled steel joist sections in place of the pressed steel frames used previously.

As demand increased even further it became apparent that the market existed for a chassis of original design, rather than for adaptations of existing designs.

One particular point which required special study involved the driver's cab, for this had always been a problem area. With the old style of high-positioned, metal-panelled, wood-framed cab, the crane boom had to be stowed for transit over the cab roof. For greater stability and safety, a lower boom position was required, and this led to the adoption of twin cabs set either side of the boom. Although this design provided for a more horizontal boom position during travelling, it did result in a rather cramped and sparse cab for the driver.

With the introduction of the new Foden low line transit crane chassis in 1959/60, a whole new aspect was given to crane carriers; here was a sensible layout which gave the driver a full-width cab with a view uninterrupted by the crane boom, for he was

1

2

1. *Light type of Oleomat crane mounted on a Willeme 6×6 cross country carrier unit.*

2. *The ex military Thornycroft 'Amazon' cranes were very popular in the postwar years and many are still at work after 40 years of use.*

now seated well below the underside of the boom.

The new design proved popular. One customer, Ruston Bucyrus, further improved on it, however, and chassis for carrying their cranes were specified with this special cab. A considerable number of these chassis, known as 45RBCs, was produced.

The low line chassis was produced in two basic types – 6×6 and 8×6 – for lifting capacities of 30 tons and 40 tons respectively, although 6×4 and 8×4 were also supplied if requested.

The engine was either a Leyland 680 of 200 bhp or a Cummins NHK 200 of 212 bhp, and the drive was via a Foden 12-speed gearbox (four-speed with epicyclic over- and under-drive ranges). The largest customer for the chassis was Ruston Bucyrus, but considerable numbers went to Jones Cranes, Thomas Smith, Priestman Bros and Demag. Fewer chassis were supplied to Ransomes and Rapier, Newton-Chambers, Wilhag and the South African Foden distributor.

Probably because of their chunky size, dump trucks have been very popular with the diecast metal model and toy producers.

TRUCK MODELS

Cranes and tipping trucks have been a staple part of the model scene for very many years, and today the choice of good models is better than ever. There are many good diecast models on the market which will adequately furnish a model construction site in fine style

Most boys at some time or another must have enjoyed playing about with a model dump truck in a heap of sand. When one is young the facility for loading up the model truck and better still tipping out the contents has yielded endless hours of enjoyment. Closely allied to the dump truck has been the excavator or loading shovel, for again this type of toy or model provides plenty of scope for the playful handling of sand, soil or stones within the confines of an imaginary quarry, and in a child's mind this is boundless. The mobile crane has also provided the means for something approaching realism, as the model trucks can be loaded with all the miniature logs, girders, barrels or sacks.

Naturally the models used during the early days tended to be of the large tinplate variety which could withstand the rough treatment meted out by the often not too considerate youngsters. Later on one usually graduated to the diecast metal or plastic variety, which came in a smaller scale but incorporated greater detail and realism.

Often the trucks were used in connection with a model railway layout, so that plenty of transhipment of the loads could take place. One major drawback of the finer scale models was their reluctance to perform well in the sandpit type location, with frequent jamming of the 'works' and perhaps even getting lost in the garden 'quarry' forever!

With advancing years and a greater appreciation of fine scale models, however, their prototype manipulation does not involve undergoing the rigours of overscale aggregate, and they are acquired for the collection aspect rather than to be used in model locations. It is true that some are bought in order to add realism to an otherwise sterile-looking circle of model railway tracks, but a large proportion of good quality (and highly priced) models are destined purely for the display cabinet.

Such has been the state of the model collection hobby in recent years that some models never even leave their boxes, for as they disappear from the makers' lists so they become more sought after and a rise in price takes place, particularly if in mint boxed condition. Some of the models are (or become) more 'collectable' than others, and this appreciation takes place in several ways. Very early models are naturally more scarce than those made more recently and therefore they command high prices; but some comparatively modern models also enjoy very high prices because they were in production for a very short time or were produced for a special market, such as for export or a particular customer.

The production of model trucks for special promotional campaigns has increased wildly in recent years. Some have been made by the regular established manufacturers, and in other instances individual diecasters have specialized in this kind of work. Some of the promotional models are marketed or issued by the company who built the original vehicle upon which the model is based, such as the truck manufacturers DAF, Volvo, Scania and Bedford. In other cases, a model or a series of models is produced for a large-scale user of the particular vehicle or item of equipment, and these would be faithful reproductions of the original but in the paint scheme or livery of the customer. Sometimes the promotional model is merely a standard production item with the customer's name merely stuck on with a transfer, whereas at the other end of the scale it can be a highly detailed and individual model of the particular customer's fleet.

Because of their rarity the promotional models are very much sought after by collectors. Sometimes the models are merely boxed as with the regular series models, but in some instances the company carrying out the promotion will attach the model to some other piece of office gimmickry such as a calendar, cigar lighter or ashtray.

Because of their complexity and capacity to be furnished with all kinds of moving parts, specialized vehicles and construction equipment have received due attention from the modelling world. When one is young the idea of a working bulldozer, scraper or loading shovel immediately sets the fingers twitching; and this does not diminish at all with advancing years, although the emphasis then shifts to a more visual appreciation of the diecaster's art and one's ideas of actually 'playing' with the model are moderated by the possibility of damage and the depth of one's pocket!

There is no doubt that the skill of the patternmaker, diecaster and moulder reaches its peak in some of the fine scale models of such items as tower cranes, cement pumpers and other site equipment. It is true that some amount of

Just a few models from the vast collection of Ron Wilkins of London.

compromise creeps in when it comes to introducing an element of operation to some of the models, for it is necessary to provide threaded feet for the stabilizing jacks and knurled wheels for the elevating drums on a crane carrier; but these are small concessions in order to achieve the added realism of a model which carries out most of the movements possible with the original.

Another important aspect of model trucks and equipment is that of a common scale. Many of us have at one time or another cursed a certain manufacturer for having produced otherwise perfectly good models save for the variance in scale. When trying to create a model environment or diorama fits of anger can arise when it is discovered that the excavator and the dump truck are just not compatible, owing to wide variations in scale. Luckily, this state of affairs has been recognized by some manufacturers, who have striven to produce a whole range of vehicles and equipment to a common scale. What is all the more laudible is the fact that several unconnected firms market models to a similar scale, therefore making the choice of compatible models even wider.

Another bone of contention among the serious collectors-cum-modellers has been the type of wheels used by some manufacturers on their models. In some cases a wheel of similar diameter is used for a variety of models even though the wheel and tyre sizes of the originals are dissimilar. This is usually common practice among the higher volume producers who are marketing their products in a competitive field, and where a reduction in the unit cost is made possible by the use of a common wheel size. In the rarefied air of the specialized diecast model firms the higher prices necessitated by the limited production runs can absorb the production costs of accurate sized wheels and tyres. In short you 'pays your money and you takes your choice'.

The model truck hobby is probably unique in the widespread field of modifying (in other words, taking a regular production model and altering it in some way or another to achieve a particular type). Whatever models come on to the market, you can be sure that within a very short while someone will have modified it in some way. He may want merely to repaint it in the colours of a special operator, or to discard a large part of the model merely to acquire one particular part, such as the cab.

No matter what is produced someone will always want something a little different. If a six-wheeler is marketed then someone will certainly add another axle or two. If only a day cab is issued, then soon somebody will want a sleeper. Where a model is sold with a tank body, you can be sure that someone will want to convert it to an aircraft fueller. So it goes on, and this is probably the most fascinating part of truck modelling, for it provides far more enthusiasts with the opportunity for what one might call semi-scratch building than ever before. With such a wide variety of models produced today in both diecast metal and plastic, in complete form or in kit, there are infinite possibilities for the would-be scratch builder who perhaps has neither the skill nor the time to build up the whole model from scratch. By being a modifier he has the best of both worlds: on the one hand a wide variety of basic models from which to make a start, and on the other an even wider choice of modelling materials to help him with his conversions.

For the converter who wants to construct his own bodies, chassis, towers, booms, etc. there is marketed a wide range of plastic card in various thicknesses and shapes. Add to this the parts which can be obtained from other damaged models or from unwanted kits, plus any leftovers from previous conversions or rebuilds, together with materials obtained from non-modelling sources such as discarded packaging, artwork or handicrafts, and there you have a limitless supply. Any good modeller worth his salt will soon accumulate a box of bits and pieces for future use, although a word of warning is necessary here: do not keep everything! It is no use hanging on to every little offcut or you will soon be buried under the pile. No, try to be selective, and above all have a filing system so that there are separate boxes or locations for such things as axles, wheels, fuel tanks, lights, air tanks and window glass. Sort the other material into common lots such as flat, angle, tube and channel.

Another claim for tidiness comes from the place of work. If you have your own workshop, fine. Even in these circumstances, however, a clean up after every session will help. For the man who has to use the kitchen table or a cupboard in the corner, tidiness is the watchword. Some form of system for tool storage is as important as filing away the materials. Again, everything used frequently should be close at hand and properly grouped for ease of access. Keep fine drill bits in a rack if possible; transparent boxes are useful for the tiny bolts; do not leave sharp modelling knives rolling about in boxes with other tools or materials; lock the cabinet or room if small children are about and do not work 'unsociable' long hours.

To single out which firm makes the best models would be attempting the impossible. Often the idea as to which are the best models is purely and simply in the mind of the purchaser. Whereas one modeller will gladly pay a considerable sum for a model and then let it sit in its box in a cupboard, another will search out the most reasonable buy and then smartly cut it up and create something entirely different. To use the old phrase, it is 'horses for courses'. The first man will be quite happy to accept the model knowing it to be the best obtainable, whereas the second will expect much more from his purchase and not be content until it is resplendent with its extra axles and finished in its fluorescent mauve.

Interestingly, some of the older firms in the business have produced some good models in their time, whereas other more recent manufacturers have striven to give the discerning modeller or collector something a little better or at least to provide greater variety. Old established companies, like Dinky Toys in both England and France, have produced some good models from the point of view of both the avid modeller and the

Three diecast models of crane carriers by Dinky Toys and Gescha.

diecast collector. Similarly Corgi, Matchbox, Marklin, Lion Toy and many others have been responsible for the issue of good models although originally marketed for the toy trade. Good condition items are seized by the collectors, but the converters also avidly gather up the damaged ones from the boxes on the floor of the various swap meets with a view to future individual models.

Although it was the smaller scales which attracted many manufacturers, the serious model enthusiasts are usually more pleased to get something in the 1/43rd or larger if possible. Scale is another aspect of modelling which often divides its followers. To some, 4 mm scale is far too miniscule, whereas to others the idea of having a room literally full of 1/25th models is nothing less than claustrophobic. Except for the fine plastic kits which are available in the larger scales, diecast metal holds sway in the small HO/OO area and is particularly prevalent in the popular 1/43rd size. Many find this scale ideal for it combines an acceptable level of detail with a manageable size with regard to storage. Several firms produce models in this scale, which is of great help when mixing models on a diorama or when carrying out conversions and alterations. The appearance of some plastic kits in the same scale has been a boon to those who wished to build American prototypes without recourse to the large 1/25th scale kits.

1

2

3

1. Diecast models of dump trucks and a face shovel by NZG, Gescha and Dinky Toys.

2. Although quite good models on their own, items such as these would look infinitely better if they were stripped of their gloss paint and repainted in semi-matt with a little dirt added for realism. Better still would be to add small details such as mirrors and set them into a site diorama.

3. The NZG cement pumper is one of several models available of this prototype. After careful study of a full size vehicle it should be possible to add small details in order to promote a highly finished model.

ERTL, AMT and Airfix have been busy in the plastic kit world for some time now and have many followers.

The world of the diecast metal kit is somewhat smaller both in scale and volume. The majority are produced by much smaller companies or even individuals who issue models in very limited numbers. This is for various reasons, among which are the smaller demand for highly specialized models, the sheer weight of metal required for some scale models and the fact that dies do suffer from repeated use with a resulting loss of fine detail.

The bulk of the market at present revolves around good quality diecast metal models, although some of these do resort to plastic moulding for items such as tilt covers and other fittings. Firms such as Gescha, or more recently Conrad-Gescha, NZG, Siku, Solido, Marklin, Ziss, Mercury, JRD, Lindberg, LBS, Vilmer, Schuco, Tekno, Eligor and CIJ, to name but a few, have all produced models which are avidly collected. Whereas a few years ago there was a limited choice which embraced the more or less regular items such as dump trucks and cranes, this has been expanded into a wide diversity of models including such feats of casting as long and delicate crane booms, cab details and items of running gear. Now we can get tall tower cranes, accurate crane carriers and even asphalt spreaders!

ACKNOWLEDGEMENTS

The authors would like to thank all those companies and organisations who have helped so readily in the preparation of this publication. The level of assistance received has varied widely and most of the manufacturers listed in the Index are responsible for the photographs used in the book.

We would like to mention the particular help received from George Wimpey Ltd, Shell UK Oil, British Petroleum Ltd, the Detroit Diesel division of General Motors, Fodens Ltd and General Motors Scotland.

INDEX

Figures in italic refer to page numbers of illustrations.

AEC *23*, 74
Atkinson 77, *147*
Aveling-Barford 27, *42*, 75, 84

Baja 65
Bedford *46*, *47*, *133*, *135*, 154
Belaz *58*
Berliet 72, 74, 136, *139*
Bray *35*
British Leyland *53*, 75, 84
Bussing *55*
Butler Bros. 108

Caterpillar *11*, *25*, *40*, 78, 79, 80, *81*, 84, 108, *123*
CCC 148, 150
Clark *37*
Cline 125, 128
Crane Fruehauf 77
Cummins 74, 78, 80, 81, 85, 108, 128, 141, 151

DAF 154
Daihatsu 62
Demag 151
Deutz 138, 150
DJB *18*, *38*, 84, *114*
Douglas *86*, 150

Edbro *100*
Euclid *24*, *26*, *76*, 78, 79, 80, 81, *123*, 128, *129*

Faun 74, 78, *110*, *122*, 150
Fiat *59*, 72
Fiori *36*
Foden 6, *18*, *42*, 72, 74, 85, *95*, *112*, *113*, *114*, *144*, 150, 151
Ford *2*, *45*, *48*, *54*, 65, 88, *100*, *101*
Foremost *53*, *119*, *122*, *134*, 140, *140*
Fuller 84

Gloster Saro *95*
GM Allison 74, 84, 85
GM Detroit Diesel 78, 80, 81, 83, 84, 108, 128, 137, 140
Goodyear 141
Gottwald *143*, 148
Grove *145*

Haulamatic 84
Hayes 106, *109*
Heathfield 84
Hewitt 38
Hy-Mac *24*

Jeep 58, 60
Jones 148, 151

Kaelble *21*, 74, 75, 85, *121*, 124
Kenworth 74, *83*, 85, 106, *123*, 125, 137
Kirkstall 148
Kockums 78
Komatsu 78
Kraz 72
KW-Dart 96

Land-Rover 58, 60
Lectrahaul 78, 80, 83
Leyland *91*, 96, *124*, 151
Lockheed *130*, *141*

Mack *12*, *19*, *31*, *70*, *71*, 72, 79, 85, *106*, 125, *125*, 128, 148
Magirus Deutz 6, 71, 72, 76, 136, 138
MAN *30*, 72
Marion *29*
Marmon-Herrington 65
Mercedes Benz 60, 72, 78, 85, *93*, *117*
Michelin *85*
Mogilev *73*
Mol 136, 137, 138
Moxy 27

Newton-Chambers 151
Nissan 62
Nord-Verk *32*

OAF 72
Oleomat *151*
Oshkosh *4*, *7*, *41*, *50*, 136, *139*

Pacific 106, 108
Perkins 84, 150
Perlini *14*, 78, 84
Priestman 151
PRP 136

Rapier *147*, 148, 151
Reynolds-Boughton 65
Rockwell 85
Rolls-Royce 84
Rubber Railway *30*
Ruston Bucyrus *29*, 148, 151

Saurer *43*
SAVIEM *58*
Scammell *17*, *72*, 74, 75, 136, *137*, 138, *138*
Scania 72, 154
Schmidt *56*, *61*, 65
Sisu *107*
Steyr-Daimler-Puch 60, 62, *64*, 65
Stonefield 60

Struver *93*, 94, 96
Subaru *64*
Suzuki 62

Tatra 72, 85
Terberg *15*
Terex *14*, *23*, *26*, 78, *78*, 79, *79*, 80, 81, 83, *114*, 128
Thew-Lorain 148
Thompson Bros. *88*, *91*, 96
Thornycroft 75, *151*
Thos. Smith 151
Thwaites *34*
Toyota 62

UAZ *58*
Unimog *36*, *57*, 60, *61*, *62*, *117*

Volvo *22*, 72, *103*, *106*, *111*, *115*

Wabco 78, 80, 81, 83
White 96
Wilhag 151
Willème 136, *151*

ZF 84, 85
Zweiweg *116*, *118*